REAL WORLD
SELF-DEFENSE

A Guide to
Staying Alive in
Dangerous Times

Jerry VanCook

Paladin Press · Boulder, Colorado

WARNING

The information and techniques presented herein can be dangerous and could result in serious injury or death. The author, publisher, and distributors of this book disclaim any liability from any damage or injuries of any type that a reader or user of information contained in this book may incur from the use of said information. This book is *for information purposes only.*

Real World Self-Defense:
A Guide to Staying Alive in Dangerous Times
by Jerry VanCook

Copyright © 1999 by Jerry VanCook

ISBN 13: 978-1-58160-044-5
Printed in the United States of America

Published by Paladin Press, a division of
Paladin Enterprises, Inc.
Gunbarrel Tech Center
7077 Winchester Circle
Boulder, Colorado 80301 USA
+1.303.443.7250

Direct inquiries and/or orders to the above address.

PALADIN, PALADIN PRESS, and the "horse head" design
are trademarks belonging to Paladin Enterprises and
registered in United States Patent and Trademark Office.

Photos by Gary Campbell

Visit our Web site at www.paladin-press.com

Contents

PART TWO
Fight Time

PART THREE
Training

Foreword

Changing Gears

The Evolutionary
Nature of Survival

The ever-increasing violence in today's world makes it high time for a book such as *Real World Self-Defense.* Over the many years that I have been involved in tactical training, I have met many highly skilled individuals. In attempting to capture the essence of true personal protection, some have taken a purely martial arts approach, while others have adopted a more paramilitary position, utilizing the many forms of weapons.

While both strategies have their strong points, few instructors have combined the two, and only a handful have attempted to look into the core concepts of the human mind—both the positive impulses that can be used for motivation and the negatives that can sabotage our efforts—that lie behind their endeavors. Among those few who have, even fewer can articulate these concepts in an understandable manner when asked to do so. Mind you, these teachers can shoot well, they can fight with the best, and they are intelligent people; they have mastered the *physical* side of things. But they have not captured and shared what personal self-defense—and personal survival—are really about on an intellectual, teacher-sharing level. That is Jerry VanCook's gift.

In simple, easy-to-understand layman's terms, *Real World Self-Defense* can help the reader understand the vital necessity of a working personal protection system and the correct mind-set for the world of today and beyond. Putting aside all hollow ritual and the many "false gods" of combat, VanCook has tackled the job of procuring a realistic program to deal with the problems unique to contemporary society, be they unwarranted attack or the irrational legal aftermath that too often follows.

VanCook has laid things out in no uncertain terms. He knows from personal experience what works on the street and what doesn't. His common sense and sophisticated simplicity appeal to the inner self of every man who has "seen the elephant" and lived to tell about it. Likewise, the novice can learn from this book. It keeps the focus on the goal of survival and bypasses the commercialization and politically correct nonsense that clogs the arteries of many current "experts" and their academies.

Real World Self-Defense streamlines the efforts of those individuals seeking answers to the violence we are all experiencing in today's society. VanCook has spent many years in the martial arts, law enforcement, and the study of weapons, and through this experience he discovered that many "truths" currently being touted are more suited to sport or art than personal combat. When violence broke out during his many years as an undercover cop, he was masquerading as a civilian. These experiences offered him an opportunity to test techniques under "real world" rather than "dojo" conditions. It also meant that his goal was no different from yours and mine—he was doing his best to survive against some of the most vicious characters on the planet, not attempting to subdue and arrest the perpetrators, as most officers are. And make no mistake—the two goals are *not* the same.

The good part about all this is that now Jerry VanCook is sharing it all with you, the reader, in this book. It is his strength as a writer to deliver this vital message in such a powerful and concise manner. Entertaining, fun, and tactically on the mark, this is a book that I believe you will thoroughly enjoy—and learn from. It can increase your survival skills far beyond the local martial arts studio or firing range.

Remember, fellow tacticians, the mind is where the battle is always first won or lost, and this book can help you achieve a vital edge through both a physical and intellectual understanding of the dynamics of human conflict.

I have known Jerry VanCook for many years, and I am proud to see his informative work on close-quarters battle and personal protection come to print. Jerry's opinions on things parallel many of my own. The world has been misled in many ways, and this book will help all people regain a sense of personal worth and confidence.

Personal self-defense goes beyond the law or even the Constitution. It is a birthright, and a God-given right—an instinct-based reaction to a threat—and it has kept our species alive for centuries. Let *Real World Self-Defense* get you up to cruising speed and beyond. Let's shift gears, my friends; it is the nature of combat, and it is time to *evolve*.

—Master at Arms James A. Keating

Real World Self-Defense: A Guide to Staying Alive in Dangerous Times is dedicated to the memories of

Leon Spencer Cook, 1920–1998
and
Lois Fern Melka Cook, 1925–1988

Thanks, Mom and Dad. More than one "shrink" has told me I'd be doing time right now without you.

Preface

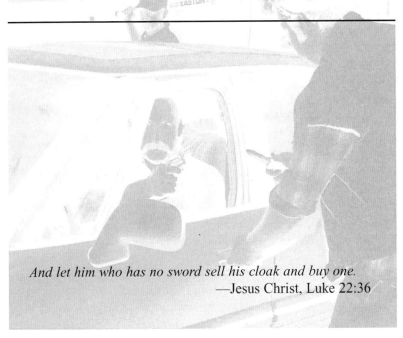

And let him who has no sword sell his cloak and buy one.
—Jesus Christ, Luke 22:36

Gone are the days when life was simple. Today, any intelligent person's self-defense package must comprise not only the ability to punch, kick, and shoot, but a basic understanding of criminals, courts, police, and politics as well.

As we near the end of this millennium, two distinct transformations are taking place on our streets and in our courts. First, while the majority of violent attacks are still committed by family members or assailants otherwise known to the victim, random attacks by strangers are occurring at a much higher rate than ever before. Blame drugs, blame gang initiations, blame whatever you'd like. The bottom line is this trend promises to continue.

Second, we must add a new problem to the equation—our own government. Both federal and state regulators continue to erode the individual's right to defend himself through new statutes restricting

There was a time when young men faced each other in a sort of 20th-century version of the *code duella*. Friends on both sides stood back and watched, not interfering unless one party appeared to be suffering severe injury.

weapons and the misinterpretation of established and time-honored laws relating to personal protection. Self-serving prosecutors are jumping on the "politically correct" bandwagon, which means that men and women who would have once been heralded as heroes for defending themselves, their loved ones, or their property, now serve prison time for such noble acts of courage. Perhaps this destructive reversal in the attitude of lawmakers and prosecutors comes from an honest-but-naive belief that gun control and other self-defense restrictions curb crime. Perhaps it is only part of a larger, more sinister effort to create a docile populace. The philosophy behind this trend is an interesting subject itself but does not fall within the parameters of this book. Nor is it of very high priority when some street punk is bashing in your head with a baseball bat, cutting your throat, or raping your wife. Survival is, at that point, not just the highest priority; it is the *only* priority. What becomes important is the victim's ability to escape both attacks—the initial onslaught from the assailant, and then the aftermath of a justice system that is often not just.

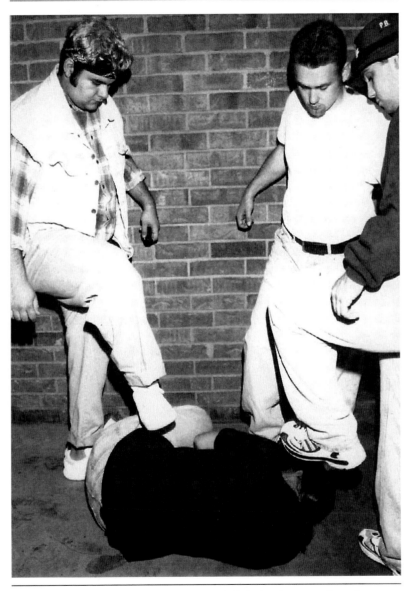

Any *code duella* remaining in the 21st century is in isolated areas and usually among friends who have arguments. This gang attack with no mercy is a far more likely event today.

The purpose of *Real World Self-Defense* is to help the reader learn to do just that.

One of the few memories I have left from a freshman zoology class I took many years ago is the fact that human beings, like all animals, have two instincts that drive them. First, and most deeply rooted, is survival of the individual. In other words, it is natural for all animals, including the kind that walk upright, to do everything possible to avoid death. This instinct extends to include those we love, and is perhaps even stronger when the individual finds a son, daughter, mother, father, or other loved one in jeopardy. The stories of men and women sacrificing their own lives for those they love are countless.

The second most innate instinct is survival of the species—the sex drive. What I find amazing today is that while survival of the species is still going strong, social pressure seems to have destroyed the will to fight in many people—even when it is essential to individual survival. Concurrently, some of the same people who cannot, or will not, fight for their lives continue to lead sexually promiscuous life-styles in an era when sleeping with the wrong person can be as deadly as any bullet. Have the two basic instincts somehow reversed priorities in their minds?

In the America of today, it is far more fashionable to be a victim than a victor. Why? I suspect that in some ways it is a subconscious attempt on the part of some individuals to show the world that they are so "sensitive," so "caring," so "politically correct" that they couldn't possibly, under any circumstances, raise a hand against a fellow human. But there is another reason as well: this mind-set lifts a tremendous burden from the shoulders of those who do not want the responsibility of taking charge of their own safety and that of their loved ones. It is a ready-made excuse for cowards.

Since people of this mind-set claim they could never hurt anyone, they find preparing themselves for self-defense not only distasteful but aimless. Most glide through life with Lady Luck as their co-pilot and finally die of natural causes at a ripe old age, still true believers in this reality of their own creation. But others less fortunate fall victim to predators whose sole existence depends upon their ability to seek out such lambs of society. This is when the created reality crumbles, and the "caring individual" learns a very painful lesson too late: he is not quite as caring as he thought he was. He is not the gentle pacifist he has professed to be. He wants to live; the survival instinct, though it may have been repressed, has still been passed down to him from his warrior ancestors. Now he wants to fight back so he can live on.

But he doesn't know how.

Some of you reading this may be becoming uncomfortable with, or even angry at, my words. That's a good sign. The fact that you have stuck with me this far means your head isn't inserted so far up your nether regions that it can't be extracted. In the following chapters, I hope to convince you that you can become an efficient fighter without turning into a feral beast. The trick, you see, is very simple. *You never fight unless it is absolutely necessary.*

The Christian Bible says there is a time for peace and a time for war. All other recognized religions have similar teachings. Christ said, "Turn the other cheek," and these are words I do my best to live by. But He also spoke the words that begin this introduction, and I believe He meant for them to be followed as well. God knows the difference between a slap to the cheek and a life-threatening situation, and I believe He expects us to handle each appropriately. A slap is merely an insult, and returning it is revenge rather than self-defense. A true assault that may leave you dead, paralyzed, or otherwise seriously injured is a different matter altogether. We must respect the life God has given us enough to fight for it, even when that means taking the life of an assailant if that assailant leaves us no other recourse.

My hope is that this book will be useful to both the beginning and experienced student of defense, to civilians, police officers, and soldiers alike. To those of you who are already seasoned warriors, perhaps my experiences can shed a new light on your own understanding, as I know yours could mine. It is not you whom I addressed when I spoke of those who might be growing angry at my stark view of combat—you were the ones nodding your heads in agreement. God bless you all. While some of the following pages may seem elementary to you, it is my sincere hope that I can present to you my own understanding of self-defense in today's world, and perhaps even open your eyes to some aspects you had not considered, as I am certain you could open mine given the chance. Keep up the good fight, pass the word, and teach others to fight back when unjustly assaulted—be it on the street or in the courtroom. Self-defense is a normal, moral act. So teach your family, friends, and students practical defense against both physical and legal marauders.

To the new personal defense student, I would say this: never assume that just because someone holds a particular job or wears a certain uniform or title that he is a warrior. There are plenty of martial arts instructors, soldiers, and cops who are—but there are at least as many that have never truly understood or embraced the warrior mentality. Conversely, I know stockbrokers, college professors, accountants, and preachers whom it would be very unwise to attack.

I chose to write this book in first person because that is the only method of narration that permits the intimate writer-reader relationship I hope to achieve. I want you to feel as though I'm sitting in your living room or on the other side of a coffee table talking with you. I hope you will see me as a real, live human being just like you, complete with my own strengths and weaknesses, tolerances and prejudices, insights and ignorances, rather than just some obscure, distant and detached writing machine. If you can do that, then you will absorb what I say far more efficiently. Then, you may accept or reject each of my ideas in accordance with your own discernment. And that—using your own common sense and judgment in mastering the practical and very unromantic subject of self-defense—is the major underlying theme of this book.

Another important thing to keep in mind is that when I say "he" or "him," I am referring to women as well as men. This is grammatically correct (if not politically so), and to attempt to do otherwise makes for clumsy, boring, and downright silly writing that distracts from the text. Staying politically correct these days is such a crapshoot that I don't even bother trying. You never know what's going to offend some people; all you can count on is that it will be something different this week than it was last. If my use of the masculine form offends anyone, perhaps it's time you came to terms with another of life's realities: sexism, like racism, is a matter of how you treat people, not what you call them. Prejudices dwell in the heart and soul—not in words.

My mother and father considered each other equals. Therefore, I grew up considering men and women equal—but only in the ways anyone can be equal to anyone else: in the eyes of God and in the way they should be treated by others. In all other respects every human being on the face of this planet is different, and *unequal*. Some people are smarter than others, some are stronger. Some are ambitious, others lazy. Some people are attractive while others are physically ugly. These are cold, hard facts of life, and we can pretend they don't exist if we like, but that will not change the reality. There is no level playing field, and no amount of idealistic wishing is ever going to create one. You must grasp, and accept, this truth if your self-defense program is to be effective.

During the years I've taught people to defend themselves, I have found that men and women usually have different motivations for learning to protect themselves. They also have different obstacles to overcome in order to learn. Men are concerned with getting hurt, but they're at least equally worried about the blow to the masculine ego that comes from losing a fight. Men also, more often than not, enter a training course with preconceived ideas and some less-than-perfect fighting methods that must be overcome before proper techniques can be learned.

Women rarely have these problems; their motivation and obstacles are different. Consciously or unconsciously, the possibility of rape is almost always the catalyst for a woman's interest in self-defense. There are exceptions, of course, and a violent ex-husband or former boyfriend quite often fits into the equation somewhere. Women rarely worry about looking silly or weak as much as they worry about actual physical injury. They are far more realistic in this respect, and, without the male ego to work through, are usually much easier to teach.

In today's society, it is as proper for a woman to study self-defense and develop the warrior mind-set as it is for her to hold a job, apply her makeup, change a flat tire, or breast-feed her baby.

Personal defense is neither masculine nor feminine, and the warrior mind-set and ability to defend do not distract from a woman's femininity. My wife is a perfect example. She is all woman but one of the toughest-minded human beings I've ever known. She has the warrior mind-set in spades. Another way of putting it is what I often tell my self-defense classes: "If you break into my house, do yourself a favor and do it when I'm home. You'll have a better chance of survival than if it's just Becky there."

Just one of the things I find attractive in a woman, I guess.

While there are a few very muscular power-lifting and body-building females out there, the average woman is simply not as strong as the average man. Therefore, the woman who attempts to match strength with a male attacker has lost before she begins, and for that reason her systems and strategies for practical self-defense cannot be based on brute force. Of course, this applies equally to the male who must defend against a stronger male. Add to this the fact that society's predators do their best to choose victims whom they perceive to be weaker and we see that the person attacked, regardless of sex, is almost always at a disadvantage in the strength department.

My use of humor as a teaching tool should in no way be misinterpreted. In the following pages we will often be looking at life and death issues, and you don't find many more sober subjects than that. But in close to 30 years of teaching I have learned that a good instructor must also be an entertainer if he is to keep his students' attention. There's another reason I use humor: I like it. I don't know about you, but personally I don't like to go even one day without a good laugh. It's one of the things that make life worth living—and defending, so you can laugh again tomorrow.

I will also be mixing in some of my personal experiences as examples. These begin in my childhood days when, for whatever reason, I often felt compelled to be the one who confronted playground bullies who picked on smaller kids. Other anecdotes come from my days in law enforcement, as a martial arts instructor, and sometimes as a younger adult who seemed to have an attraction to life's seedier establishments. This, too, is done as an aid to understanding. It is not in order to brag about how smart or tough I am, and the rather embarrassing nature of some of these examples should more than prove that out.

The actual fighting techniques we will explore in *Real World Self-Defense* are simple and easy to learn—at least at the most rudimentary level of understanding. They are techniques I know personally to be effective because I have used them myself in physical encounters. But this is primarily a book of concepts, not another of the many texts on the market today filled with page after page of photos and step-by-step directions on defense in specific situations. There are plenty of those already. Some are good, others are bad, and, as in all aspects of life, most fall somewhere in between. The worst of the defense manuals are those that take the "he does this so you do that" approach. This is an exercise in futility, since, in reality, "he will *never* do that," and if he does, he will not do "it" in the same way you trained for him to do it.

The good self-defense books may approach the subject from slightly different angles, but they all have two things in common: they recognize that each self-defense situation is unique in and of itself, and they advise taking the simplest path possible to solving the problem. They promote the same basic, easy-to-learn techniques that have proven throughout history to be useful under the intense level of stress produced by life-and-death confrontations.

Just as there are no new plots available to fiction writers, there are no self-defense techniques that have not been around for thousands of years. Good novelists, therefore, tell the old stories in new ways, in new settings with new characters, and they tell the stories from their own singular viewpoints that make the old stories seem new. When the writer does his job well, he trips a switch in the reader's brain, and the reader then relates the plot, theme, or emotion in the book to an experience from his own life. That's when the reader looks down at the page, takes a deep breath, and says to himself, "Man, that's good." He may have encountered the same plot or theme in a hundred other novels, and it is safe to say that every writer he has ever read has tried to establish that emotional connection. But for some reason, this time, things just "clicked."

A good self-defense instructor, whether in person or through a book, video, or any other medium, does much the same thing. Different students respond to different stimuli. Different personalities find certain instructors, or certain types of instruction, easier to comprehend than others do. There is nothing new in this book—just old ideas and truths expounded by me from my personal point of view. It is my hope, however, that I might relate them to you in a fresh way— in a way that will trip that switch. If I am able to connect with even one person who pauses, looks at the page, and says to himself, "Hey, that's right—I never really thought about it that way before," then I will consider my effort worthwhile. And if that connection leads to an innocent person—who might otherwise have become a victim—overcoming his assailant and escaping injury and the potential legal nightmare that can follow the use of force . . . then I will consider *Real World Self-Defense* to have been a tremendous success.

If you come to something in this book with which you disagree, that's fine; no one is telling you that you must totally accept, or reject, every single aspect of my philosophy. But I would ask that you at least consider those things that seem to contradict your own views. I have found in my own self-defense studies that the ideas that initially make me bristle most often concern aspects of self-defense that I have not completely worked out in my own mind yet.

Now, please relax, open your mind, and read on.

I want you to be nice . . . until it's time to stop being nice.
—Patrick Swayze as "Dalton" in the movie *Roadhouse*

Acknowledgments

Real World Self-Defense would have been impossible without the help of the following people: Bill Addington, Col. Rex Applegate, David Axe, Steve Barron, Bax Baxter, Sam Blumenthal, Chris Bowers, Mark Bray, L.D. Brown, Bob Burnett, Aaron Clark, Chuck Clark, David Collins, Debbie Compton, Becky Cook, Jed Cook, Leon and Lois Cook, Sid Cookerly, George Davis, Steve Dick, Steve Duncan, George Englebretson, Bram Frank, Casey Furr, Kari Grant, Kit Givan, Gene and Zelma Gott, Pat Harkin, Morris Hart, Ed Hasbrook, Michael Heenan, W. Hock Hochheim, Bob Howard, Mike Hronopulos, Bobby and Deborah Hunter, Michael Janich, Catherine Johnson, Ted Jones, James A. Keating, Joyce Laituri, William H. Mays, Kendra McClenney, Mike McQuay, Darla Minor, Feroze Mohammed, Jamey Montgomery, Jerry Oven, Karen Pochert, Johnny Quarles, Aaron Reil, Eric Remmen, Leslie

Ribera, John Saucier, Tibbie and Virginia Shades, Bruce Siddle, Tony Stephens, Shawn Shropshire, Walt Tatum, Lynn Thompson, Thomas Jerry Turpin, Bari VanCook, Lynette Wert, Dwayne Williams, Steve and Jo Wilson, and R.B. Yadon.

Finally, a very special thanks to Gary Campbell for his tireless efforts behind the camera.

All of you played some part in making me what I am. So to various degrees, you're all to blame.

Introduction

I have not followed the paths of other men. I have lived without benefit of a teacher and by my own devices I became master of myself, and thereby master of the sword and the brush, never differentiating between any of these "arts."
—Miyamoto Musashi
Go Rin No Sho (A Book of Five Rings), c. 1643

One of the very best friends I've ever had is a fellow martial artist named Chuck Clark. I have the utmost respect for Chuck, and he's one of the few of my contemporaries I truly believe deserves the title *shihan*, or master. Chuck once told me I was a warrior-poet-priest. It embarrassed me when he said that. But later it dawned on me that he hadn't said I was a *good* warrior-poet-priest—just *a* warrior-poet-priest. After I realized that, I decided it pretty much fit.

No, I am not the world's best warrior. But I think like a warrior, act like a warrior, and, therefore, like the man who walks and talks like a duck, I must be one. I have never made the best-seller list with any of my books, but I am still writing, and making a decent living at it, and therefore I must be a writer—or as Chuck put it, a poet. I am a Christian, and although I do not stand on street corners forcing religious tracts into the hands of passersby or attempting in any other

1

way to push my beliefs off on people who aren't interested, let someone show an interest and I am delighted to discuss my faith with them. In a sense, I suppose that makes me a priest.

Miyamoto Musashi, the 17th century swordsman who wrote the words above, speaks of swordsmanship and the art of painting as if they were the same thing. They are. So are self-defense and writing. You see, beneath the surface there is a connection between all things.

When I write a novel, in plotting the story I use concepts that first became clear to me through martial arts training. When I train for self-defense, and when I must actually put my self-defense training into practice, I transfer perceptions I first acquired through writing into physical form. I used strategies that had their origins in football plays when I was an undercover police officer, and things I learned in college drama classes I later applied to working crime scenes when I became an investigator.

Lessons that come from one area of life can be transferred to all others. I don't just mean obvious examples, like the fact that learning to correctly angle a basketball off the backboard so it goes through the hoop can teach you how to sink the eight ball in the side pocket on a pool table. Such things are part of what I'm talking about, but only at the most rudimentary level. If you pay attention, allow yourself to become open to and develop a sensitivity to the interrelationships of life, you'll begin to perceive more subtle correlations between activities that seem unconnected on the surface. Like how training for a hundred-mile bicycle ride can relate to grieving over the death of a loved one. Or how the same principles of changing the filter in your air conditioner can be applied to reading a book. I'm not trying to turn into some mysterious oracle with all this; it's really very simple once you allow yourself to see it. Teach yourself to look for the ways all things relate to each other rather than just seeing their differences.

What this means for our purposes here is two-fold: 1) life, in seemingly unrelated ways, has already taught you more self-defense than you probably realize, and 2) you should strive for a personal system that integrates all aspects of defense into one package—one mind-set—rather than viewing them as separate entities, such as gun fighting, knife fighting, unarmed combat, and so on. You see, you may be called upon to put more than one item from that package to work at the same time. Like fighting off a sudden attack with one hand while you go for your gun with the other. Or reaching for your gun, finding that your assailant has pinned your arm to your chest, and being forced to access your knife with the other hand. If you have spent all your training time thinking, "Now I am practicing pistol, and when I'm finished I'll work on knife and then unarmed defense," you will not have developed the proper mind-set to survive. Integrate the different components, both in your mind and in your training.

As well as a warrior-poet-priest, I am a teacher. I teach self-defense seminars and creative writing classes, and I teach through my writing itself. Regardless of the subject, or whether I'm instructing in a gym, classroom, or at a computer keyboard, I have a philosophy about teaching: I don't really believe anybody can teach anybody else very much, if anything. I believe good teachers understand that they should really view themselves more as "guides." About the best they can hope to accomplish is to point the few sincerely interested students in the right direction—and then encourage them. Teachers can be an inspiration by providing examples of how specific knowledge has benefited them personally. But they can perform demonstrations, assign exercises, and lecture until they turn blue in the face and it won't do a whole lot of good to the student who isn't passionate about learning. Once in a while, teachers say something, see a face in the class suddenly brighten, and know they connected with that specific student. But those moments are few and far between, and they are only the tip of the iceberg of true learning.

You see, like Miyamoto Musashi, any student who really wants to master a subject must become his own teacher.

Consider for a moment any area in which you yourself are well educated, perhaps even expert. This may be chemistry, needlepoint, medicine, aircraft mechanics, martial arts, scrimshawing, or any other subject that applies to you. Did you learn most of what you know from teachers? No, you learned it on your own. If you were lucky, you had a teacher or two who recognized your interest and aptitude and inspired you to educate yourself. They taught you everything they could in class and may have even spent extra time with you outside the classroom. But what they actually taught you is minuscule compared to your overall knowledge of the subject today. What the good teacher did was spark an interest that caused you to create your own self-study program; they whetted your appetite to delve deeper into your chosen discipline—deeper than any class could ever hope to go. And if you had a really good teacher he incited you to be creative in your approach to learning. He encouraged you to question current wisdom rather than blindly accept it and never to sell your own ideas short just because someone else's opinions came first.

Let's look at Musashi again for a moment. He is known as *Kensei*, or "Sword Saint," throughout Japan because he is reputed to have been the best sword fighter in the history of that country. But was he really the best? Who knows? He didn't fight every one of the millions of swordsmen Japan has produced over the centuries, so maybe yes, maybe no. Looking at it realistically rather than romantically, the odds are actually against him. Many, many Japanese have become great swordsmen throughout history, and any number of unknown warriors probably could have defeated Musashi. But that's not the point. Even if he really was the best, he was not the *only* great swordsman. There were many others, and they all had their own techniques and strategies; they just didn't write them down. Many of their tactics were so different from Musashi's that they actually seem to contradict his teaching. Does this mean they were wrong? I don't think that can be said with any authority since each man's individual system worked for him.

The fact is that you, like Miyamoto Musashi, can teach yourself anything you want to learn, including practical self-defense. And just because you are not the best fighter in the world does not mean your ideas are not sound, or that you do not deserve to hold your own opinions, which may even oppose current wisdom. If only the man deemed best at anything was allowed his convictions, there would be only one view on each subject and nothing—not art, science, or anything else—would ever develop and grow.

Before you become your own self-defense teacher it helps to

have a background in a traditional fighting art like karate or aikido or boxing or wrestling. But it's not absolutely necessary. And make no mistake; self-education is not the route for everyone. It takes far more commitment, diligence, and self-discipline to be your own teacher than to go to a dojo three to five times a week and allow things to be spoon-fed to you.

In the paragraph following Musashi's quote that opened this Introduction, he went on to write, "It should be understood that without the assistance of a teacher many roads become open to a practitioner, some on the correct path and some on the incorrect path. It is not for everyone to be without guidance; only a few—and they are exceptional—can make a journey to wisdom without a teacher."

Let me take that one step further. Each individual is also different at different times in his life. When I began martial arts training, I would have been lost without a teacher. But there came a time when I needed to pursue my fighting education on my own, and at that point I became equally lost trying to do so under the limitations imposed by following an instructor. Some people are not of the personality that they can ever walk the road to self-education all on their own. But those who can *must*. This is the only way they can find "the way" that is right for them instead of simply becoming imperfect clones of their teachers. And even those who decide to stay with an instructor will never reach their full potential until they learn to think for themselves rather than follow him blindly.

I have another very good friend and excellent martial artist we'll call Pete. Pete has devoted his life to the way of the warrior since early childhood, and now, in his mid-50s, heads a very respectable organization. But like all of us, he is not perfect, and his childhood was hardly ideal. A bad relationship with his father made him easy prey during early adulthood for an unscrupulous martial arts "guru." We'll call the "guru" Eric, since it starts with the same letter as evil and is therefore highly appropriate. Eric was one of those megalomaniacal teachers who, unfortunately, possess enough charisma to create a mindless cult-like atmosphere within their organizations. You've seen them—little mini-Hitlers; Jim Jones in a gi. Anyway, still searching for a father figure, Pete was taken advantage of and abused for years by this man who posed as friend and mentor. When he attempted to resist outrageous demands on his time or monetary contributions to the "mother school," he was made to feel disloyal by this manipulative bastard. (I try to save words like that for special people who really deserve them.) I had trained with both men and could see that Pete's abilities and understanding of his art had long ago surpassed Eric's. Pete didn't need the man; he just thought he did.

The break came when Eric pushed too hard, and Pete had finally reached a point where he recognized the unhealthy situation. And ladies and gentlemen, it was beautiful to watch. Now that Pete was finally free to pursue his martial arts education on his own, his physical expertise and spirit began to soar. And perhaps most beautiful of all, he and his father came to understand and accept each other before his father's death. Like Miyamoto Musashi, Pete became a master on his own.

You will probably never reach Pete's level of expertise, even if you dedicate your life to martial studies the way he has. I haven't, and I don't expect to do so. But it's not necessary that you reach that level just to adequately defend yourself. I assume, however, that like me, you would like to become "as good as you can get." Well, you will never achieve that goal until you understand that even if you remain in formal training, your teacher must eventually become no more than an assistant instructor. Sooner or later, you must be your own primary teacher.

None of this, of course, means you should never listen to what teachers and other fighters may tell you. I have learned much in dojos and gyms all over the world, and I value the time I spent in them. Self-education is not so much a change in where, how, or with whom you train as it is a change in attitude. Like so much else we will be discussing, it is a mind-set. It is, in some ways, simply taking charge of your own life rather than handing the reins over to someone else. This is a bigger responsibility than many people are willing to accept, for it means that each new concept and technique you encounter, whether it originates in your own mind or comes from someone else, must be critically analyzed. And it is you who must critique it, because you alone can decide if it has merit. And even if it does, you will likely need to modify it to fit your own physical, spiritual, and mental uniqueness. But this is what the true warrior (or any intelligent and self-confident person for that matter) does. He does not blindly accept anything just because the person promoting it wears a higher belt, has a fancy title, or has been at it longer. This is why not all skilled martial artists are warriors.

For much of my life, I had a relationship with my father that was something of a cross between the relationships Pete had with both his father and Eric. Dad was a very successful person at everything he did. For much of my life, I attempted to emulate him, always falling short—and always being left with the feeling that I would never be as "good" (whatever that actually means) as he was. When he gave me advice, I took it, and tried to do whatever I was trying to do the way I thought he would do it because I knew his words must be only slightly short of the Gospel. More often than not, I failed. It's important to remember here that, unlike Eric and his self-serving relationship with Pete, my father loved me and was doing the very best he could to help me. The results, however, were just as destructive.

Then, one day, I'd had enough and just flat gave up. I told myself that I would never be as good as my father, I would always disappoint him, and there was nothing I could do about it so I might as well just get on with my own life as best I could. I completely quit listening to his advice, began making my own decisions and doing things my own way, and for a short period of time took a perverse delight in going against many of the axioms Dad had, with the best of intentions and fatherly love, drilled into me over the years. As the old saying goes, I "threw the baby out with the bath water."

But strange and unexpected things began to happen almost immediately. In short, I became more successful at everything I attempted. So for a time, I decided my father's "way" was wrong. Then, gradually, I began to realize that the way he viewed and handled things was not wrong—for him. They were just wrong for me. So rather than reject everything Dad had tried to instill in me, I began to pick and choose, then modify his principles to fit my own personality. When this concept finally sank in, and I threw out the "either-

7

or" attitude, I found I attained even better results in my endeavors, and my accomplishments multiplied tenfold.

I suspect this is a transition between father and son that is not unusual. But I also suspect it is one that occurs far earlier in life for most men. I was well into my 30s when I finally grew up.

Keep me, my father, Pete, his father, Eric, and whatever similar personal life experiences these anecdotes have conjured up for you in mind as we begin looking as some basic concepts. If you are new to self-defense, don't just sit there reading and nodding and taking my word for everything just because I got this book published. And if you're an experienced fighter and have decided you don't like what I have to say so far, I would still challenge you to do the same thing. You have more than two options; you don't have to consummately accept or reject. You can also partially accept and modify. And 99 percent of the time, partial acceptance and modification is the best answer.

If the blind lead the blind, both shall fall into the ditch.
—Matthew 25:14

8

PART

1

LET'S GET READY TO RUMBLE

1

Attitude

The Warrior Mind-Set is Everything

In war you cannot afford the luxury of squeamishness. Either you kill or capture, or you will be captured or killed. We've got to be tough to win, and we've got to be ruthless— tougher and more ruthless than our enemies.

—Capt. W.E. Fairbairn
Get Tough, 1942

To say Margaret is beautiful would be a vast understatement. She has black hair, olive skin, and those mysterious Mediterranean features that catch the eye of just about every man who sees her. But one night, about 15 years ago when she was still in college, she caught the eye of the wrong kind of man.

Margaret was on her way back to her dorm after studying late at the university library. Her arms were full of books, and her mind was on the math test she'd be taking the next morning as she walked over a bridge that spanned a lake on campus. She had walked this same route every night for weeks, and becoming a victim of attack was the last thing on her mind.

The rapist, too, knew she walked this path at roughly the same time every night. So he hid in a grove of trees on the other side of the lake and watched her cross the bridge.

Before she even knew what was happening, the books flew from her arms and Margaret found herself on the ground, being pulled into the trees. The rapist was already ripping at her blouse, but she was so stunned she had no idea how to handle the situation. Then, suddenly, something clicked in her brain. Without really even knowing what she was doing, she found herself biting and clawing and scratching and screaming. One of her thumbs happened across the would-be rapist's eyes and she dug it into the socket. Now it was his turn to scream, and that gave Margaret a chance to roll out from under him, rise to her feet, and kick him in the head. That worked so well she did it again. And again, and again, and again. Margaret's initial shock, which had turned to fear, now became a righteous anger. What right did this pervert have to lay his hands on her? What made him think he could get away with such a thing? She kicked him several more times in the head and ribs, then took off running and didn't stop until she got back to her dormitory.

Today, Margaret is a third-degree black belt in tae kwon do. But at the time of this attack, she had never had a self-defense class of any type in her life.

What Margaret did have, however, was the warrior mind-set.

When W.E. Fairbairn wrote the words at the beginning of this chapter, Great Britain was expecting an invasion by Nazi Germany at any moment. Fairbairn, who had survived more than *200 gunfights* as a Shanghai police officer, had returned to England along with E.A. Sykes to teach the British Home Guard to defend their country. He was trying then to do very much what I am about to attempt—make people who have rarely, if ever, experienced firsthand violence understand that a mind preconditioned to survival is the single most important aspect of self-defense. You see, defending yourself from murder, rape, or robbery is nothing short of a war. A small and intimate war, perhaps, but a war nonetheless.

What Fairbairn refers to as "toughness" and "ruthlessness," however, must not be misinterpreted as "going wild." Don't think of a rabid dog when visualizing this—think more of the vicious but well-controlled and calculated tactics of a lion. A high level of fear and anger is likely to be present, particularly if there has been sufficient warning that an attack is inevitable. But these emotions cannot be allowed to overcome judgment. No single aspect of defense guarantees survival, but those who keep their heads and at the same time focus their natural emotions along a constructive path of defense gain a tremendous advantage.

Col. Rex Applegate, an American Office of Strategic Services (OSS) command officer during World War II who was closely associated with Fairbairn and Sykes, explains this in his book *Kill or Get Killed* when he speaks of mental balance: "The most basic fundamental of all is that of balance. Mental balance, or stability, is a state of mind that is necessary before physical balance can be achieved."

My interpretation of what the colonel calls "mental balance" here is that in a violent self-defense situation we must each, in a sense, become two people. One of "us" must be subjective, letting our natural fear and outrage provide the fuel for our defense. But the other one of "us," the objective "us," must keep that fear and outrage from going wild and spending itself on unproductive action. All of our efforts must remain focused on our ultimate goal—survival. And if we can break the mental balance of our opponent while retaining our own duality, we gain a tremendous advantage.

What we need, first and foremost, when under attack, is the warrior mind-set. This was once also called the "killer instinct," but that term is now used by everyone from athletic coaches to business executives and has lost much of its true meaning. The word "warrior" itself is in danger of going the same route, with nonsensical expressions like "peaceful warrior" and "mental warrior" and "political warrior" infesting our language. A true warrior goes to war, be it in uniform for his country or wearing Bermuda shorts when attacked on the street. A warrior is a man or woman who is willing to physically fight when there is no other recourse, not one who knows how to strategically negotiate a business deal.

There was a time in human history when our ancestors did not question the morality of their predatory disposition. If they wanted something, be it the choice cuts of a recently killed woolly mammoth or the tribe's most desirable cave woman, they killed anyone who stood in their way of getting it. As civilization took root, most human beings began to realize that fighting and killing for selfish reasons was an immoral act, and they began to reserve such actions for defending themselves, their loved ones, and their property. This has been the stance of moral human beings ever since—that violence should be reserved for appropriate defensive purposes. Unfortunately, we are still surrounded by a good many immoral bipedal animals who do not play by these rules. Even more unfortunate is the fact that a large proportion of our society likes to pretend that the predators simply don't exist. They have now gone beyond restricting violence to appropriate circumstances into a realm in which they claim that violence is always an incorrect response. "Violence is never the answer" is a mindless cliché parroted by many these days. In reality, *counter*violence is sometimes the only answer.

The tennis player who sees his opponent on one side of the court and slams the ball to the opposite corner is exhibiting only a watered-down version of the killer instinct. He may, or may not, also have the true warrior mind-set that would enable him to look another man in the eyes, then cut the throat beneath those eyes if that's what it took to stay alive. But this athletic or business-type "killer instinct" can be a place to start in learning the proper mental attitude for self-defense. If you've ever played sports, particularly contact sports, you've already gotten a glimpse of what the warrior mind-set is all about. Remember that linebacker in high school who used to smile when he drove his helmet into the gut of the opposing team's running back? He was getting pretty close to it. He might have been the kindest, most considerate individual in the whole school when he stepped off the field, but there was a man inside those shoulder pads who knew there were appropriate times to use violence.

Our linebacker's conduct provides us with an example of another important consideration in today's self-defense: playing by the rules of the game. He tackled the running back with every pound of power he could generate, but he didn't reach under the man's face mask and strangle him after the play was over. And he reserved his controlled violence for the appropriate time and place—during the game, on the playing field. He didn't run down the halls between classes, arbitrarily tackling everyone he met.

If you want to survive an attack *and* stay out of jail afterwards, this "playing by the rules" concept is something you must constantly keep in mind as you develop your defensive skills and warrior mind-set. The rules for self-defense are more complex than those of a football game. Football games are played under rules determined before the game begins, and they remain consistent. If a football player so desires, he can even study the rulebook before the game. Each self-defense situation, however, has its own unique set of rules. You won't get a chance to become acquainted with them until the "game" begins, and they may change several times during the encounter. In order to protect yourself from both bodily harm and the legal aftermath that is likely to follow even a justified response, you must recognize and play by the rules.

Different situations demand different levels of response. There is a big difference between dealing with your brother-in-law who gets drunk and behaves obnoxiously at a wedding and waking up in the middle of the night to find a strange man with a gun standing over your bed. In the same sense, we must differentiate between a true attempted rape and a date who just has a hard time keeping his hands to himself. You have a legal, but, more importantly, a *moral* obligation to handle different levels of threat differently. The man in your house may have to be killed. Your brother-in-law (no matter how much you've always secretly believed he deserved death just on general principles) probably just needs a firm escort outside where he can get some fresh air and sober up. A firm "Stop it!" or even an elbow in the ribs should end the problem presented by the impertinent date, but if it escalates to a true rape situation, a more violent response may become necessary. The law and what, again, I believe to be far more important than the law—morality—always demand that you use the least amount of force necessary to get the job done.

The study of self-defense comprises many strange aspects that at first seem almost contradictory. One of those is the fact that the techniques which are easiest to learn are often the most deadly. This holds true both in armed and unarmed combat. The easiest shot to make with a firearm is the one aimed at center mass of the human body—where the most vital organs are located. With a knife, a thrust

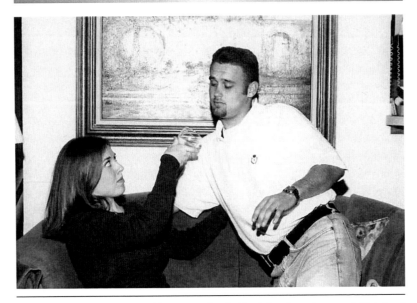

Low-level threats, such as this over enthusiastic date, do not warrant high-level responses. If a glass of wine in the face is enough to cool this young man off, that's where it should end.

to the same center mass is one of the easiest techniques to learn; it is also the most fatal. In unarmed defense, striking with hands and feet is far simpler to master than the more complex arm bars, come-alongs, and other restraint tactics that enable you to control your attacker without doing serious damage.

Several problems arise from this phenomenon. First, as already alluded to, killing or seriously maiming your brother-in-law or the overenthusiastic date would be an improper response. Another problem is that simply learning to shoot a gun, use a knife or stick, or employ empty-hand defensive techniques is absolutely worthless without the will to use them. Even worse, continually seeing yourself progress in a training program can instill a false confidence and set you up for a very rude awakening someday when you actually do find yourself in a life-or-death encounter. Many remarkably well-trained police officers, soldiers, and martial artists have learned too late that this essential psychological development—the warrior

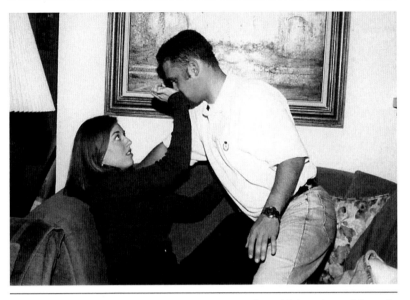

If the threat level escalates, the response must escalate with it up to, and through, deadly force if that is the only answer.

mind-set—had not matured along with their physical prowess. In short, they choked when the chips were down.

One of the favorite arguments of gun-control advocates is that citizens who possess firearms are more likely to have them taken away by their attacker than to successfully defend themselves with their weapon. This will undoubtedly be the only time you ever hear me even partially agree with the gun-grabbers, so listen closely: unlike most of their biased propaganda, this particular claim contains at least a little bit of truth. It is the conclusions drawn from this statistic that are flawed. The fact that a citizen *has* a gun is not what causes the gun to be taken away. That result stems from the citizen's not having the correct mind-set to go with the gun. Invariably, a gun is taken from and used on its owner because the owner was not mentally prepared to do what he needed to do—shoot another human being. It doesn't matter if you've won 500 full-contact karate tournaments, shoot Distinguished Master at the firing range, and are

Possessing a weapon without the proper mind-set to use it is more dangerous than being unarmed. Now, in addition to a knife and baseball bat, these attackers now have this man's gun.

holding a bazooka in your hands. If you do not have the warrior mind-set when you need it, all training and weapons are worse than worthless—you have, indeed, just armed your own murderer.

Developing the correct mind-set is not easy in today's society. Among other problems, our own government discourages it, preferring docile, obedient, easily managed little subjects to free-thinking citizens. Note how police public relations officers (more often than not minions of management who are no longer cops but politicians) advise citizens to handle violent situations such as car-jackings. "Do not resist!" they stress over and over. "Your wallet and your car are not worth your life!" Well, most of us hardly need to be told this; we would gladly give up all of our material possessions if we could be certain it meant we could go on living. But can we be certain? Do we know that we won't be killed anyway as soon as the carjackers get our money and automobile? Such vermin are far more famous for impulsive action than they are for rational thinking. Sometimes they

Being prepared and responding quickly is a necessity in self-defense. Shown here is a man who was ready for this car-jacking. Let's hope he doesn't miss the little goblins approaching the vehicle from the other side.

kill people just because it's fun. And getting rid of witnesses is a thought that will always cross their minds, whether they follow through with it or not. Do you, particularly while under the stress of having a gun shoved in your face, feel competent to divine the exact point where the attack will terminate? You'll have a split second to do so. Keep in mind while you answer this that top psychiatrists specializing in criminal behavior have been trying to do this for decades—unsuccessfully. Police spokesmen, self-defense instructors, and anyone else who gives "blanket advice" to never fight back should be thrown behind bars themselves, and a society that promotes such passive behavior might as well put signs on their cars that read, "Wimp on board. Take my car, rape me, and kill me. I'm yours for the taking."

Our government even discourages the warrior mind-set in its own police agencies. Each bureau or department must have a few warriors within its ranks, since situations periodically arise that cannot be handled with pencils, paper, or computers. But on a day-to-day basis the warrior-officer is watched suspiciously by his bureaucratic superiors. Cowardly officers, who always manage to find some way to stay out of the line of fire, attempt to give warrior-officers the image of knuckle-dragging savages. With very few exceptions, law enforcement agencies that stand behind their officers when violence is mandatory are a thing of the past. Most departments, bureaus, and other institutions would far rather one of their men got killed than face a lawsuit.

Regardless of whether you're a cop, soldier, or civilian, if you haven't already done so, now is the time to take a hard and realistic look at the inner workings of your brain, emotions, and soul. Do you have what it takes to look into the eyes of a man pointing a gun at you and then pump two rounds from your own gun into his chest? If that doesn't stop the threat, can you add another pair between his eyes? Can you cut his throat if that's what you must do to save your life or the lives of your loved ones? Can you, like Margaret did, gouge out an eye if necessary? If your answers were yes, read on. If you decide the answers were no, ask yourself another question: "Am I willing to develop that mind-set?" If you answer yes to this one, you, too, should continue reading.

If you answer no again, you have bought the wrong book. Take it to a used bookstore and trade it in for one of the many politically correct self-defense books that are so popular today. Learn to blow a whistle or activate a loud buzzer when the 300-pound methamphetamine monster attacks you. Be assertive and yell "No!" in his face. Put all your faith in that cell phone whose advocates would have you believe it will freeze murderers and rapists in their tracks the moment they see you draw it. Or take the "new age" self-defense path—when the bullets begin to fly, just surround yourself with one of those all-protective "auras of goodness and light." I believe quite strongly in the power of prayer. But if you go this route, you'd better believe in it even more than I do.

I read a book several years ago by a woman who had ridden her bicycle around the world. Before setting off on this adventure, she had attended one of these "new age" consciousness raising semi-

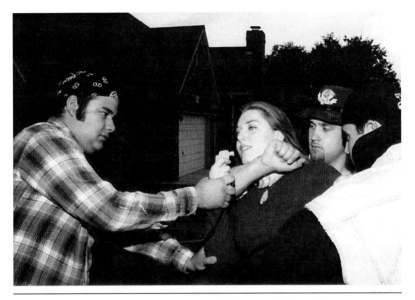

Nonviolent solutions to violent attack are rarely, if ever, sufficient. This young woman *almost* got the whistle to her lips. But what good would it have been if she had?

nars—the type, I suppose, where they make you stay awake until you finally break down crying and tell them humiliating secrets. In any case, she learned that violence was never the answer—reason and "light" would always protect her. So she learned to encircle herself with this "aura of goodness and light" I just mentioned, and it kept her bicycle from getting hit in heavy traffic all over the world. (Watching the road might have had something to do with that, too.) Unfortunately, however, it did not prevent her from getting raped. Her attacker was one of the many mongrels of today's society who simply will not be reasoned with, and he seemed not to notice the magic "aura" surrounding her. Or perhaps he did, but possessed his own even stronger magic, which enabled him to penetrate this protective shield as the Klingons sometimes manage to do with the starship *Enterprise*.

This woman, rather than learn from her mistake, remains a true believer who would make Eric Hoffman proud; she credits her magic aura with the fact that she was not killed after the rape. The fact of the matter is she's alive only because the rapist was just a rapist—not a rapist-murderer. If she had fought back successfully, she would still be alive, and she would not have been raped either. This "new age" self-defense stuff would be funny if it wasn't so dangerous to the people who swallow it.

Passive virtue is great most of the time, but let's never kid ourselves when it comes to serious self-defense; simply being a good person alone won't stop a determined murderer or rapist. I'm all for goodness, and if you do your best to be honest, moral, and kind, this "aura of goodness and light" emanates from you on its own—you don't have to go to some seminar and have them hocus-pocus it out of you. The best example of true "goodness and light" I've ever seen is a woman who has been one of my dearest friends since high school. She's the kindest, most gentle human being I've ever known, and she risks her life every day to run a program for inner city kids in one of Los Angeles' most gang-ridden areas. She *cares*. She tells me she has angels who protect her, and I pray that she's right. I'd never say such a thing wasn't possible, and if anybody ever deserved a whole army of heavenly guards, it's her. But in my case, I've pretty much decided God expects me to take part in the fight, too.

In short, I worry about her. Good people get hurt by bad people every day.

I am guessing that while you are not perfect, as I am not, you are basically a good person. Well, good people do not want to do serious bodily harm to others. (A desire to hurt people means that you are not a good person any more.) Unfortunately, a significant number of nefarious self-defense instructors and writers have picked up on this fact and seem more than willing to take advantage of it these days. They present programs that play to this desire not to hurt others by convincing their students and readers that there are alternate, nonviolent methods that will always enable them to escape injury. They sell a "magic" nonviolent solution to nice people who want a nonviolent solution so badly that they convince themselves one exists. The duped are persuaded to believe that the magic whistle, the magic cellular phone, or the magic assertive

"No!" will make even the most determined assailant disappear into thin air. Such programs instill a very comfortable "now-I'm-safe-and-I-don't-have-to-hurt-anybody" false confidence that make those who take them seriously victims in waiting.

A recent book of this nature even made the best-seller list. I won't name it here for fear that some of you might disregard my advice and not only waste your $22.95 plus tax but take some part of it seriously. Its author, who owns an executive protection company and protects the rich and famous, "writes down" to readers as if they are children, and his elitism and hypocrisy are evident throughout the text. He condemns private firearm ownership in one breath, then talks about his own armed personnel in the next. His entire message is so transparently self-serving as to be laughable, and it can be summed up in two sentences: "Don't buy one of those nasty old guns because you're not smart enough or brave enough to use it. Hire me instead." Once you've gotten past all the dangerous delusions in this book (and the shameless name-dropping of the stars for whom he works), it becomes evident that the author actually does know what he's talking about when it comes to the subject of fear and how it can be made to work for you rather than against you. But overall, his book is a prime example of these programs that play to good people's basic resistance to using violence—even when counterviolence is the only realistic answer.

Nonviolent reactions to straight-on, hard-driving, hell-bent-for leather attacks simply do not work. If they did, soldiers would carry whistles and cell phones instead of rifles and hand grenades. The nonviolent approach is effective only at the drunken brother-in-law and "handsy" date level of threat we looked at earlier, and this level is actually more nuisance than true threat. The two-legged animal that is fully committed to hurting you is going to shove your whistle down your throat to keep you quiet. The cellular phone may go up another part of your anatomy and stay there until it can be surgical-ly removed once you're in the hospital anyway. Don't worry about calling the ambulance—the police will do that for you when they respond to your 911 call—if you had time make one—minutes, if not hours later after your assailant has left the scene. The self-confident

Defending oneself from deadly attack is a down-and-dirty business. You must be willing to gouge eyes out or cut someone's throat if necessary. Repugnant, you say? The author agrees. But being the victim of rape or murder is even more repugnant.

and affirmative "No!" you practiced so diligently in class will not be heard above the animalistic grunts and groans of the murderer who is plunging a knife in and out of your chest.

No matter how much you'd like it to be otherwise, defending your life is a down-and-dirty business, and the "downer" your attacker gets, the "dirtier" you must get. There is simply no other way. If you do not already understand that, the sooner you do so, the sooner you will be able to put practical self-defense into practice. While 99 percent of your life should be spent being a kind and gentle person, if a killer attacks you, you will not survive unless you kick in that warrior mind-set and become a killer yourself.

A few people, I suspect, are born with the warrior mind-set; I have observed five-year-old judo students who were as aggressive as Navy SEALs the first time they stepped onto the mat. Most of us, however, must develop this way of thinking. I believe I probably began to develop the warrior mind-set somewhere in junior high school, and I would credit sports—particularly football—with getting me started. You see, deep down inside all of us lurks that prehistoric caveman-predator. What this means to us in modern society is that, as long as you don't use violence unless it is absolutely the only recourse, there is a secret little part of you that will sort of enjoy it when you do. Maybe it's no different from knowing we did a good job at something, but I suspect it's really a little deeper and darker than that. While decent humans have learned to restrict their predatory instincts, those instincts haven't disappeared from the species. The urge to prey is still within us all, and while we must keep it under control, we should also learn to draw on it when we need it. Defending yourself is natural, it's human, and it's the right thing to do.

Call it what you will—the warrior mind-set, the killer instinct, or simply the willingness to injure or even kill if that's what is necessary to preserve your own life. *It is the single most important facet of self-defense.* It is far more important than being a marksman, a master bladesman, or an expert in hand-to-hand fighting. Remember my telling you that after Margaret's near-rape she began to study tae kwon do and is now a third-degree black belt? Well, ironically, the instructor who promoted her to that level, although very pretty to watch, is nothing more than a coward at heart. I'd pick Margaret to back me up over him any day. Don't ever forget that at the time Margaret was attacked she had no training, and the warrior mind-set saw her through on its own. My good friend Hock Hochheim calls this "fighting first, systems second." It's what Fairbairn had in mind when he entitled his book *Get Tough.* The warrior mind-set alone may see you through.

But it's far better to have both the warrior mind-set and realistic self-defense training. So let's move on.

The most basic fundamental of all is balance. Mental balance, or stability, is a state of mind that is necessary before physical balance can be achieved.

—Col. Rex Applegate
Kill or Get Killed, 1942

2

When your Heart Goes Bump in the Night

Psychological and Physiological Changes During Combat

They spake not a word;
But like dumb statues or breathing stones
Gazed each on other, and looked deadly pale.

—Shakespeare
Richard III, III

In other words, they froze. They choked. They were too scared to act.

It takes courage to act when under physical attack, or when facing any kind of danger for that matter. But courage is often misunderstood. Many people confuse courage with the absence of fear, and this is not only incorrect, it can be very destructive to the person who faces danger, experiences fear, and therefore concludes he is a coward. Danger + Fear = Cowardice is a faulty equation, and placing belief in it can, in and of itself, turn you into one of Shakespeare's "dumb statues or breathing stones."

There is great truth in the old saying that "the only people who never get scared are fools and liars." Courage is not an antonym for fear; courage is the ability to force yourself to do what you know must be done in spite of the terror. It's the possession of a mind that can force into action arms that want to hang limply at your sides and legs that feel as if they each weigh 500 pounds.

To extricate yourself from a current danger, you must often expose yourself to what may be perceived as an even greater danger. If a man is holding a gun in your face and states that on the count of three he intends to blow your brains out, the courageous thing to do is force yourself to at least attempt to take the gun away from him. If you fail, the result may be that he kills you on the count of one or two instead of three. But it's amazing how many people in situations like this choose to wait out such a death, as if that extra second or two of life might bring the sound of a bugle followed by the cavalry riding over the hill to save them. To put this simply, if he is going to kill you anyway, does it not make sense to at least *try* to save yourself? Does it not make sense to die, if you must, as a person who attempted to defend himself and left this world fighting rather than sniveling?

I am not saying that inaction is always wrong. H.G. Bohn wrote in his *Handbook of Proverbs*, 1855, "Courage ought to have eyes as well as arms." Sometimes doing nothing for the moment is the best solution. Let's take the same man with the gun, and rather than have him announce that he is about to kill you, let him say, "All I want is your money. Give it to me and I won't hurt you." Assuming, of course, that his body language and all other aspects of this specific situation lead you to believe he is telling the truth, doing as he demands is probably a wise decision. But the operative word is *decision*. Doing nothing should be the result of definite calculation on your part; it should not come from the fact that you are so petrified you *can't* do anything.

There is another way of looking at courage, and sometimes I believe it is even more accurate—at least for those with the warrior mind-set. Often, I wonder if warriors aren't just more afraid of having to live with themselves after behaving like recreants than they are of any physical danger. There is an old French proverb that seems to support this idea: "Courage is often an effect of fear."

Fear is going to come to most of us when we face danger, and the level of fear, at least in a rational human being, is directly proportionate to the level of threat. What is important is how we handle the symptoms of the fear we experience. Fear can totally paralyze a person, or it can be channeled into constructive actions that save lives. But before we delve deeper into this subject, let's look at self-defense in terms of two basic (and admittedly oversimplified) types of attack and the different roles fear plays in each.

First is the surprise attack. If you have prepared yourself mentally to do whatever is necessary to preserve your life and practiced basic self-defense techniques until they've become stored in your muscle memory, you aren't likely to have time to experience much fear. You will react rather than act, and it will all be over (one way or the other, and let's hope it goes your way) before fear has time to sink in. Of course, afterwards you are going to come to know that wonderful experience with which I'm sure some of you are already familiar. You come down off your "battle high," realize what just happened, and suddenly an adrenaline rush about a hundred times stronger than any you've ever experienced hits your system. Now, the threat is over and the adrenaline is no longer needed, so it has no constructive place to go. But is has to go somewhere. And it does.

You may begin to tremble uncontrollably. You may experience an intense desire to run—not away from the threat; like I said, it's over—in order to work off this sudden burst of energy. If you're like me, this fervent need for physical activity will last only until the adrenaline finds a home in your stomach. Then you'll feel like every flu you've ever had got together, had children, and the whole clan decided your stomach was the best place to settle. You may, or may not, actually throw up, but in any case you'll go home after it's all over with a different perspective on the rookie movie cops who puke their guts out while Dirty Harry Callahan goes on calmly eating his hot dog. It isn't fear that causes this reaction; the time for fear has come and gone. Nor, at least in most people, is it being "grossed out" by all the blood and guts. It's that adrenaline surge that makes you sick.

Okay, so much for the easy ones.

Far more difficult are the situations you know are coming and that give you too much time to think. For the soldier, this may be the night before a dangerous patrol in which he tosses and turns sleeplessly on his bunk. For the police officer, it could be preparing for a

In self-defense situations in which there is too much time to think, you can easily become your own worst enemy. Unless this woman has developed the warrior mind-set and gained confidence through training, her imagination will run wild as she awaits the intruder she just heard break into her house.

manhunt through the woods, knowing the suspects are armed and have already shot a cop or two. For the citizen it may be awakening in the middle of the night and hearing the noises of an intruder, slowly but surely, drawing ever closer to his bedroom. Prolonged waiting periods are not fun for anyone, but they can be a living hell for those unaccustomed to the psychological and physiological changes they will experience. The imagination has a field day. You may become so jumpy you can't stand still, or suddenly find yourself so sleepy you can't keep your eyes open. Again, like Shakespeare's "stone statues" you may freeze up all together. Extreme nausea may enter the picture because rather than after the fact, this time the adrenaline has come too soon, and it is not yet time to act.

I suppose the ideal attack, if there is such a thing, would come with the perfect amount of time to totally prepare yourself—and no more. Unfortunately, the aggressor is the one who gets to choose the playing field and kickoff time, not you. But the bottom line is, if you do not keep these reactions to fear under control, you are going to panic and do something detrimental to your survival.

Some people are more prone to panic than others, but everyone, and I do mean everyone, can fall victim to it under the right circumstances. Case in point: many years ago, after several weeks of training in a swimming pool, I took my scuba certification dive in a lake. In the pool I had experienced no claustrophobia or any of the other problems commonly associated with diving. But about 30 feet beneath the surface of the lake, I suddenly froze. All I could see was brown. I began to panic. I wanted nothing more in the world than to be back on dry land, and I wanted to be there *now*.

Modern scuba diving is a very safe sport. Little children, elderly men and women, and even people with severe physical disabilities engage in it. My equipment was functioning perfectly, I wasn't caught up in any of the trash at the bottom, and you don't see too many sharks in Oklahoma lakes. The only danger I was in came from the near-hysteria I was experiencing and the foolish actions it threatened to bring on.

So what was causing this sudden panic? At the time I had no idea, since I had been shot at, stabbed, and faced death other times without panicking. This confused me, and the confusion added to the problem. Looking back on it now, however, the catalyst for my fear is very clear. One week before that first dive, I had driven my newborn son and his mother home from the hospital. I had suddenly, for the first time in my life, taken on full responsibility for the survival of another human being. During that dive, all I could see with my eyes was brown water, but all I could see in my mind was that little face wrapped up in the blanket. How would he ever learn to throw a baseball or kick a football if I died? Who would teach him right from wrong, and how to protect himself?

There was nothing rational about my fear—becoming a first-time father didn't make scuba diving a bit more dangerous than it had been the week before. But the dramatic changes I was experiencing in my life had upset my mental and emotional balance, and, in turn, my self-confidence.

Obviously, I made it through the dive. But it took every ounce of willpower I possessed to keep from shooting straight to the surface. Instead, I forced myself to follow the scuba instructor through the water and perform the simple tasks that were required of me in order to receive my C-card. When it was over, no one but I knew the terror I had experienced. In the days that followed, I adjusted to my new role as father. When I dove next (I figured it had to be like falling off a horse—you'd better get right back on), I experienced no problems.

I tell this somewhat embarrassing tale to illustrate a point: we all have periods in our lives—days, weeks, or even months—when our confidence is not what it is at other times. These can be dangerous times, particularly if we do not recognize the symptoms, as I didn't until I was under water. But these periods of self-doubt are one of life's realities, and they must be dealt with.

Let me relate another personal experience that illustrates the other end of the spectrum. For reasons unimportant here, I have gone through a couple of periods in my life when absolutely nothing frightened me. (No, I'm not one of the liars in the old adage; I'm one of the fools.) During one of these periods I was working as an undercover narcotics investigator (which had nothing to do with the problem; it was personal), and I found myself taking some incredibly stupid chances. (Some risk is inherent in that kind of work, but I was going way beyond the call of duty in the stupidity department.) Granted, I did some of my best work during that period, but at the same time I needlessly endangered not only my own life but the lives of many fellow officers. It wasn't so much that I wanted to die; more like I just didn't care if I lived or not. In contrast, the near panic I experienced on that certification dive was a result of my subconscious perception that, as a new father, I had more to live for than I could handle.

Just as you must recognize those times in your life when you're at higher risk of falling victim to panic, you must also be aware of the apathetic periods. They are usually the result of personal loss and a mistaken belief that you have little, if anything, left to live for.

By now, I have either convinced you that I understand these problems or that I am a total neurotic. What I described are examples of extreme emotional periods in life—times when you may very well act differently than normal or, as writers and actors often say, "break character." There is a third danger which comes from a false confidence in your abilities, but we're going to cover that in detail later, so let's move on and look at the periods in your life when you're normal (or at least as normal as you get).

Even assuming you aren't under some pressure that throws your judgment out of whack, you are still going to experience some level of fear when you sense a life-threatening situation. The best study I have ever seen on battle stress is Bruce Siddle's book, *Sharpening the Warrior's Edge*. Siddle is a former law enforcement officer and director of PPCT Management Systems (PPCT stands for Pressure Point Control Tactics), a company that trains criminal justice officers and members of special warfare and special operations units. His book deals with the relationship between survival stress, escalating heart rates, and combat performance. I highly recommend it, particularly for those of you interested in a deeper understanding of the "hows and whys" of combat stress. For our purposes here, we're going to stick to the whats.

Danger causes the heart rate to go up rapidly and dramatically. Even a pulse rate of 115 will show a decline in fine motor skills (hand and finger movement, usually involving at least some hand-eye coordination). Complex skills (always in conjunction with hand-eye coordination, and consisting of a series of movements that usually involve multiple muscle groups working in conjunction) begin to decline at around 145 beats per minute, and by the time your heart rate reaches 175—forget it, they're out of control. But gross motor skills (large muscle groups doing simple tasks) seem to follow a pretty steady increase in performance as the heart rate rises.

Let's look at a few examples that illustrate these facts. Although balance and technique play a larger part in power-lifting than non-participants realize, there is probably no other sport that depends as highly on simple brute strength. The bench press, dead lift, and squat are the epitome of using major muscle groups or gross motor skills. If you've never seen a power-lifting meet, go watch one sometime. Pay attention to the behavior of the competitors immediately before they attempt a lift. They take deep breaths, they snort like bulls; some of them even yell and scream and jump up and down like madmen. They know from experience that raising their heart rate will increase performance.

Now, let's change sporting events and think of target shooters. I don't care what kind—make it bulls-eye, IPSC, PPC, or skeet. Do you see them acting like wild animals right before they shoot? Of course not. They do everything they can to relax, control their breathing, and become as calm and tranquil as possible. That's because in their sport a lower heart rate is advantageous. If you are using fine motor skills, stress and excitement are not what you want.

Are you beginning to see a dilemma here in the realm of self-defense? One exists, no doubt about it. When facing life-threatening danger, your heart rate goes up—simple fact. This may assist you in throwing a punch or swinging a club, but it destroys your ability to focus your eyes on the front sight of a firearm or "calmly squeeze" rather than "pull" a trigger. At first, this appears almost to be a contradiction of nature. Every species of animal on earth evolves in ways that make it more likely to survive, or it doesn't evolve and survive at all. Chameleons change color to blend in with their environment when they sense danger. The gazelle, when frightened, relies on his great speed to escape. Scare a grizzly bear and he'll rip you to pieces and eat you for lunch. Why? Because he can—strength, teeth, and claws are the survival gifts nature gave him.

So why, when humans are most in need of defending themselves, do their natural instincts try to make them do the very things that will help them the least?

I am not a zoologist, anthropologist, or any other kind of "ologist." But I think the answer is fairly clear. As we saw with the power-lifters, an increased heart rate does assist us in generating potency to the large muscle groups, and for most of mankind's history it was these gross motor skills that were used in survival. Clubs and rocks were our first weapons, and the more strength you had, the bigger club you could swing and the harder you could swing it. Not until the introduction of more sophisticated means of defense did fine and complex motor skills come into play. Edged weapons such as swords and knives, bringing with them the necessity of correctly aligning the point or cutting edge, began this trend. Projectile weapons, such as slings and bows, require even more complex movements, and firearms are the prime example of how today's personal defense has changed from that of our ancestors. The answer to our question, then, is that human evolution simply hasn't caught up to human technology. Perhaps someday it will, and the more stress an individual encounters the easier it will be to employ fine and complex motor skills. But we aren't going to see that in our lifetimes, so we must learn to deal with our current situation as best we can.

One of the most revealing studies Siddle looks at in *Sharpening the Warrior's Edge* is a survey of 400 police officers concerning the use of the PR-24 (side-handled baton) in actual violent arrest situations. These officers used the techniques they had learned that required complex motor skills only 20 percent of the time. In over 79.7 percent of the incidents, they employed the baton using movements that required gross motor skills.

I have been through side-handle baton training, and for political and liability reasons, the vast majority of class time is spent on the complex techniques. Instructors stress the value of these complicated moves and strongly recommend them, and most are good enough actors to do so with a straight face. (Or else they are instructors who spend all their time instructing and have never actually used the PR-24 on the streets.) Savvy officers leave these classes laughing, knowing they will never use the impractical techniques they've just wasted two days being exposed to. (Notice I did not say learning.) They realize intuitively that they have not had nearly enough time to learn the complicated movements, and what little they did absorb will have vanished from mind inside a week. A few "true believers" take this training to heart, and they are the ones I pity most. They go away from their two- to three-day seminar with that dangerous false sense of security we spoke of earlier.

We live in a real world, folks. When people—military, police, or civilian—face danger, they get scared. Then they either do that which they are capable of doing under the current stress level, or they attempt more complicated techniques, fumble the job, and get hurt or killed.

Some level of complexity is, of course, necessary in self-defense. You cannot bench press, squat, or deadlift an attacker. Even drawing a weapon or blocking a strike and countering involves multiple movements, and these movements become more difficult with life-or-death stress. So what can we do?

First, we can learn systems and concepts that rely on the *simplest techniques possible*. And at the same time we can learn to control our heart rate. Control of the heart rate, fear, anxiety—all those things that make you squirm and act like an idiot under stress—comes only with confidence. If an unarmed 3-year-old child looks you in the eye and says, "I'm going to kill you!" do you become frightened? Of course not; you are confident in your abilities to keep that from happening. But what if a six-foot, eight-inch man holding a severed head in one hand and a bowie knife in the other says the same thing? Do you take it more seriously? I hope so. This man has the capability of carrying through with the threat if you aren't up to what it takes to stop him. So what you have to do is bring your level of confidence up to and beyond that point.

Confidence comes not only from practicing your techniques but, even more importantly, from believing in what you practice. A good rule of thumb is that if you don't think a certain technique will work, you can be sure it won't. Maybe it would work for someone else, but it won't for you because you must first believe in it to give it even a chance for success. Even if you believe in it, it might not work each and every time, under all conditions. (If that were the case, we'd all learn that one self-defense technique and go home.) But you can be assured it will *never* be effective if you do not have complete faith in it.

Years ago, when I practiced and taught a traditional form of karate, we used to have a saying: "Practice your *kata* (prearranged movements much like dancing) until it's perfect; then you'll only make half a dozen mistakes when you do it on the test." You see, when you are practicing, you are under very little, if any, pressure. When you take a test on what you've practiced, the stakes are higher—you might fail. Now, take the stress of taking the hardest test you ever took in your life, any test, and multiply it by about a thousand. You're now approaching the level of stress that you will experience if you are not mentally and physically prepared for a man to sprint toward you with a butcher knife while you try to draw your own weapon. As someone once said, people who actually rise to their expectations and perform as well in combat as they do in training get medals.

The warrior mind-set and confidence in your training are the only real answers to conquering your fear. We've already talked about the warrior mind-set, so let's look at the concept of training, and we'll look at it in more detail as it applies to specific defense weapons when we come to them.

Doing nothing but shooting at paper targets will eventually make you a master shooter—of paper targets. As soon as the basics of whatever discipline (shooting, knife defense, unarmed combat, etc.) you are practicing are learned, a large proportion of your training should be conducted under as realistic conditions as possible. Actual experience is the best teacher, but provoking fights with innocent citizens so you can further your studies is frowned upon. This means you must create as much artificial stress as possible. You cannot completely replicate the stress of a real life-or-death encounter, but you can approach it in a variety of ways.

First, understand that most instructors conduct their teaching/practice sessions under ideal circumstances. In firearms instruction, for example, the student usually follows well-defined parameters set out by the range master: "Draw, fire, reholster." There's good lighting, the backdrop is taken care of for you, and there are no innocent bystanders around. In other words, nothing could be further from reality.

Let me make you privy to a few secrets about self-defense in the real world. First, there will be no referee to stop the fight as soon as there's a clear winner. It will always have just snowed, and, instead of being on a mat or tile floor, you'll be sliding around on the ice. The sun will be in your eyes, not his. It will be causing your forehead to sweat, and the sweat will be stinging your eyes to further impair your vision. The room may be 30 feet by 30 feet, like the one you trained in, but there will be chairs, tables, and other things to bump into or get hit over the head with. If guns are involved, count on innocent

A faith system is undoubtedly the one most important aspect of the warrior mind-set. There is a time for the Bible, and a time for the gun, and no contradiction exists between the two.

people also being in your way. You will always have the flu and a migraine headache, and your arm or leg will still be in a cast from falling off that ladder the week before. You will have stayed up the last two nights with a dying relative, and arthritis will be setting into all of your old football injuries.

Or perhaps your first child will have just been born.

What I am getting at is this: you will not be under ideal circumstances, and if all you have done is trained in a perfect environment, you'll be up that familiar feces creek with no oars. Introduce stress into your training. No, you won't shoot as well and your punches and kicks won't be as pretty to watch. But you'll learn to "problem solve" (and get a grasp on how to do so quickly). Next to the warrior mind-set, that's the most important aspect of self-defense.

There is one last point I'd like to make, and again for more detail please refer to *Sharpening the Warrior's Edge*. In his final chapter, Siddle writes about the value of belief systems to warriors and tells a very moving story about the death of his grandmother. He watched her, a woman of strong belief, die gallantly and without fear. I did the same with my mother, another woman of faith who, though not a warrior per se, would fight tooth-and-nail for whatever she believed in.

The value of some sort of belief system, or religion, when facing death can not be proven through scientific methods. But there is yet another old saying about there being "no atheists in the trenches." I myself am a Christian. While this does not completely erase my fears or my desire to avoid death, it softens these things immeasurably. I'm afraid I am not one to kneel each night before my bed with my hands clasped under my chin, and I seem to remember a prayer before meals only at Christmas and Thanksgiving when there is family around. But I pray silently and often throughout the day, and I am not ashamed to say that I have prayed hard and fast before inevitable life-threatening encounters when attack, and possible death, stood only moments away. I have no doubt that this aided my ability to keep my fear in check, react quickly and rationally rather than panic, and survive.

There are a couple of other little "tricks" I use as well. I hesitate to even mention them because they pale in significance when compared to the warrior mind-set, training, and belief. But I'll pass them on anyway, and hope that, kept in their proper perspective, they will help you. The first is a time-honored technique of warriors, and it's very simple: roll your eyes up and back into your head for a moment. Don't ask me to explain why this helps me relax; I just know it does. Obviously, you don't do this if there's already someone swinging a baseball bat at your head.

The second pre-battle relaxation technique I employ is to tighten my abdominal muscles as soon as I feel anxiety beginning in my chest. Then, keeping them tightened, I concentrate on my breathing. In . . . out . . . in . . . out. But, again, when I say concentrate, this obviously must not be to such an extent that you ignore your surroundings. (I don't care how tight those abs are, they won't stop a bullet or knife.) This is a very basic technique taught in yoga and many martial arts. Sometimes, my anxiety disappears. Other times, it only lessens. But I have used it so many times and found it helpful that I now do it without thinking.

Hope for the best but prepare for the worst. Train your mind all the time and your body as frequently as possible. Believe in yourself and your techniques, but most of all, have a deeper system of belief. These are the only ways to develop the warrior mind-set that will enable you to conquer your worst enemy of all—the fear that resides in us all.

He has not learned the lesson of life who does not every day surmount a fear.

—Ralph Waldo Emerson
Courage, 1877

3

Arrested for Staying Alive

Legalities and Politics in Self-Defense

The more corrupt the state, the more numerous the laws.
—Tacitus
History, III, c. 100

Originally I intended to break this subject into two chapters. One would have dealt with the legal issues involved with self-defense, the other with the politics. Doing so proved impossible. You see, in late 20th century America, politics and law have become so intertwined as to be one. Politics dictate how our laws are interpreted—with the result sometimes being a complete reversal of the spirit in which the law was originally written. All one needs to do to see how enmeshed with the law politics has become is to look at the O.J. Simpson trial. When that circus was finally over and all the clowns went home, the only thing that had been proven was that the use of racial epithets is now a more serious crime than murder.

When you think of the law in relationship to morality or common sense, never make the mistake of believing they are the same. Think more along the lines of the emblem of the Olympic Games with its connecting rings, which only partially overlay one another. Aristotle addressed this issue when he wrote, "The actions ordained by law are just actions only accidentally" (*Nicomachean Ethics*, V, c. 340 B.C.), which makes it pretty obvious this is not a dilemma unique to our times. The law is often the political tool of those with the power to use it as such, and a great amount of legislation is passed for the purpose of furthering the specific interests of the lawmakers (or their supporters) rather than for the betterment of society. Both politics and law are professions that carry with them such temptation for unscrupulous behavior that many, many of those who practice them give in to that temptation. I certainly would not go so far as to say all lawyers and politicians are corrupt (I have *one* good friend who is an honest attorney, and I've heard there's another one out there somewhere), but there is more than enough dishonesty to produce a major effect on our lives. Therefore, we must not only look at the law itself as it relates to self-defense, we must look at the way the laws are interpreted—and often distorted.

We love to spout off in this country about our jury system and how we are all judged by our peers. I will be the first to agree that we do have the best system in the world. But best, in this case, is still not really very good. In reality, our system has holes big enough to fly a C-130 transport plane through. It is far from infallible, and it cannot be counted upon to deliver justice nearly as efficiently as the average citizen who has never dealt directly with it believes. Even as I write this, somewhere in this country a judge is releasing some hardened criminal due to a legal technicality weaseled out by his attorney. We all know this happens, and we complain about it frequently. But there is another perverted side to our current political/legal atmosphere that we don't hear about as much. Somewhere today, it is also quite likely that an honest citizen who did nothing but exercise his God-given right not to be killed, crippled, raped, or robbed, will pay a price, either criminally or civilly, for exercising that right.

We also love to brag that no one in this country has the right to play judge, jury, and executioner. These duties are all to be conducted separately. But our entire criminal justice system is set up in such a way that at each level of the process one person does act as judge and jury. For those of you who might not be familiar with it, let me roughly outline this process. We'll take a hypothetical case and follow it through.

You are walking down the street, and a ragged bum (I know we're supposed to call them "homeless" these days, but this guy is a bum) approaches you and demands money in a threatening voice. You say no and try to walk past him. He pulls a knife in each hand and attacks. His arms look like the blades of an oscillating fan as he moves toward you, so you draw your legally owned and carried pistol and put two .45 ACPs into his chest. He falls to the ground, dead on the spot. Being a good citizen, you contact the police. A patrol car carrying two officers screeches to a halt, lights flashing and siren howling. After turning over your pistol, you explain what happened.

The officer in charge of the call now makes a decision. Does he handcuff you (he may very well have already done this; don't be offended, he doesn't know what happened yet, and it's for his own safety), arrest you, and throw you in the back of his car? (Quite possible.) Does he leave the bracelets off but ask you to accompany him (or even follow him in your own vehicle) to the station to write out a statement? (Also quite possible.) Or does he see this as a clear-cut case of self-defense; take your name, address, and other information; and tell you the detectives will be in touch? (Pretty unlikely, since a death has occurred.)

In many ways, the officer in charge is acting as mini-judge and jury. His final verdict on how he handles the situation will influence everything that comes later, and his decision will depend on the facts he can gather there at the scene, but also on countless other variables. Some of these variables are appropriate to his overall understanding: Do you have a criminal record? Are you a citizen of the jurisdiction or visiting? How likely is it that you could have escaped injury without killing your assailant? These are proper things for him to consider, but people who wear badges are only human; they have preconceptions and pet peeves just like the rest of us, and some of these prejudices may also enter the picture. What was your attitude? Were you respectful or contemptuous toward the officer? Were you obviously sorry this incident had to happen (note the subtle difference between *had to happen* as opposed to *happened*)? Or were you a boastful lout who now thinks he's Charles Bronson? How were you dressed? Were you wearing a business suit or gang colors? None of these things have a direct relationship to the actual event that just occurred or to whether you acted within the law or not. But they will all be filtered through the responding officer's mind and enter into his decision anyway.

It gets even more personal and self-serving with some cops. Did the cop's wife just run off with a guy who looks like you? What is the current political atmosphere in the community with regard to self-defense? How did the newspapers treat the last similar case? What is the community's feeling toward the "homeless" bums up and down the street? Perhaps most importantly, how does the present police chief or the officer's sergeant, lieutenant, captain, or whomever lords over him feel about the citizen's right to self-defense?

As you can see, the factors that can enter the picture are endless. How you are treated, and whether you are arrested or not, will be based upon a combination of what facts are available at the scene and the personal judgment of the officer. He will decide at that point whether the matter should be pursued or not, so don't tell me he isn't acting as a judge and jury; he is. Keep in mind, however, that the fact that there's a dead man lying on the sidewalk makes this a very serious situation. Even though you were 100-percent justified in your actions, that has still not been established. You are not very likely to walk away before at least being taken down to the station for questioning.

Now, let's change the particulars a little and see what happens. Instead of pulling knives, your attacker begins flailing at you with his fists. Again, you draw your .45 and kill him. You pull out your trusty cell phone (which does have a place in self-defense; it's just not the cure-all, magic elixir some believe it to be) and call 911.

This situation is a lot less clear. How big and strong and old are you? How big and strong and old was he? If you're six feet, eight inches tall, weigh 350 pounds, and play professional football for a

Your personal appearance is a big factor in how you are treated by both criminals and police after the fact. It is also an example of the contradictory nature of self-defense and the law. The young man on the right is less likely to be attacked than the one on the left. The young man on the left, however, will be viewed more favorably by law enforcement. The man in the middle is "splitting the difference."

living, you are very likely to have some serious problems—particularly if your unarmed attacker was of average size. The officer is going to look at you, then look at the ragged heap on the ground and figure one right cross would have stopped the encounter.

Let's change the details yet again. Instead of a professional defensive tackle, you are a 75-year-old man or a five-foot-two-inch woman. Now the officer is going to begin thinking that your .45 may well have been your only recourse. What all this boils down to is what's called *disparity of force*. Was shooting the bum your only reasonable defense under the specific conditions of this particular attack, or could you have escaped death or serious bodily injury with less drastic measures? Again, there are millions of variables, and obviously we cannot cover them all. The bottom line is whether, considering all the variables peculiar to your specific incident, you used more force than necessary to stop the attack.

The football player and the 75-year-old man are extremes, and you probably fall somewhere in between. But even within the extremes there are variables that could well change the situation. Was the football player limping down the street on crutches after having surgery on both knees? Was the 75-year-old man still working as a personal fitness trainer or a martial arts instructor and an expert in the defensive use of the cane he was carrying? What if the unarmed bum was screaming, "I've got AIDS and I ain't dying alone!" as he attacked? As they used to say on *Seinfeld*, "Yadda, yadda, yadda."

Again, we'll change a few of the facts. You didn't have to kill the guy. The right cross came through, or the pepper spray actually worked, or you hit him over the head with your purse. The police officer on the scene may end the thing there and then. Oh, he'll have to write a report, which will be glanced at briefly by his superiors, and may even be sent to the district attorney's (DA's) office, where it will receive another cursory look, but no serious legal problems (at least not criminal; good luck in civil court if one of the many ambulance-chasing attorneys happens to be within sniffing distance) are likely to follow. Unless, of course, the wife of the responding officer really did run off with a guy who looks like you, and he decides to make you his own personal whipping boy.

In short, the things that work for you in the actual employment of self-defense sometimes work against you in the aftermath. Being a pro football player, martial artist, or boxer—or even just being physically fit—will certainly help you defend against an attack. But it's also likely to make the responding officer wonder if you couldn't have handled the situation with less force, particularly if you are forced to kill or seriously injure your attacker, and particularly if you employ a weapon against an assailant without one. On the other hand, being in poor health, elderly, or physically disabled in some way is a detriment to your actual physical defense but a real boon to your legal defense. (You poor thing; you had to hit that man with your cane?) And, right or wrong, being female against a male aggressor will always stack the odds that you'll be viewed with less suspicion of going overboard in defending yourself.

46

Again, unless death or serious injury resulted, you are very likely to be released at the scene. The officer may even compliment your actions as being heroic. The exception will be if you are single and attractive. He will have already gotten your phone number, but he might want to take you in for questioning just to get to know you better. Hey, these guys are only human, you know.

Let's assume that you are taken to the station. Depending on departmental procedures, you may be turned over to a detective at this point. If so, it's now his turn to play judge and jury, and a whole new set of variables with regard to his likes, dislikes, tolerances, and prejudices enter the picture. Let me stress that good cops do their best to keep their personal opinions out of such decisions. But they are made of flesh and blood; they are not robots, and they are not always successful in this effort. And I hate to be the one to tell you there's really no Santa Claus, but I spent a lot of years wearing a badge, and I'd be lying if I didn't warn you that not all cops are good cops. The vast majority are very fine people, but a few are stupid, and a few others are just so downright rotten that they will not even try to set aside their own prejudices.

If the detective's decision, based on whatever he bases it on, is that you acted within your rights, you may be released after questioning but ordered to stay in contact so the case can be cleared up. (Believe me, there's so much paperwork involved in killing someone you'd think the federal government was behind it instead of the city or county.) If, however, there is reason to believe you broke the law, then your fun has just begun. If you have not already been arrested, you will be at this time. If so, you will be booked, then placed in a cell to await arraignment before a judge while the DA's office reviews the case and decides whether to prosecute or not. (New judge-jury again.)

The DA's decision will add a whole new dimension to the should-be-irrelevant-but-isn't phenomenon, but the game changes a bit here, too. The police's prime interest was whether they believed you had committed a crime. The DA will be more interested in the chances of a successful prosecution. Most DA's offices are backed up with cases all the way through Armageddon, and they operate much like an army medic separating the injured who stand a chance of survival from those too far gone to waste valuable time on. So if the evidence against you is shaky and the chances of conviction thin, you are not likely to be prosecuted. Unless . . . you are a high-profile individual, or this case, for whatever reason, has become high profile on its own. (Murder and manslaughter are almost always high-priority. Simple assault and battery without serious injury usually is not.) Or an influential party pressures the DA into prosecution. Or the DA, or one of his assistants, sees a way of using the case to further his own career. Or . . . or . . . or. . . . Again, the unknown motivations that may be present behind the scenes are legion. Each case is different, each set of police and prosecutors is different, and procedures and policies in each jurisdiction are a little different.

Plea bargaining, or "flea marketing" as many police officers call it, is now very likely to enter the picture. For those of you unfamiliar with this process, it is also sometimes referred to as "copping to lesser charges." Murder charges might be reduced to manslaughter if you plead guilty. Felonious assault could be changed to simple assault and battery. As already stated, the criminal justice system is flooded, and this is one way to get low-profile cases with "iffy" chances of conviction off the docket. But keep in mind that this can also be a little game played between the prosecutor and your attorney for their own reasons. A very "shaky" murder charge may have been filed with the specific intent of offering manslaughter for a guilty plea. (This is similar to a store that marks its merchandise above retail price with perfect intention of later marking it down and calling it a "sale.") Whether you accept a plea bargain offer or not is a personal decision. It goes against the grain of all honest people to admit to committing a crime—any crime—when they know in their hearts that they did nothing morally wrong. But each situation must be looked at individually, and each individual must decide what is best for him in such a predicament. I would not presume to make such a decision for anyone without knowing the facts of his or her case, and neither would it be my place to decide, even if I did have that information.

Assuming the decision is made to prosecute, a representative of the DA's office, which represents "the people" (the vast majority of whom, knowing the details of any reasonable self-defense case, would rather give you a medal than a prison term), will read the charges at your arraignment. Except in the most extreme cases (and defenses based on a legitimate self-defense angle rarely fall into this category), the judge will set bond. So cash in your savings, mortgage your house, sell your dog and cat if you have to, but bond out. Jails are not fun places to live—particularly for honest citizens who are not familiar with the "ins and outs" of such an institution. (Yes, the pun was intended.) During the hours, or even days, before bond becomes available and you must stay in jail, be on your guard at all times. Be prepared to fight again if necessary; perhaps even harder than you did on the street.

The next step is either a preliminary hearing or a grand jury. These are not trials, and they are not designed to determine your guilt or innocence. Their purpose is to establish that a crime has been committed and that there is sufficient evidence to believe you may have committed that crime. At a grand jury, you are finally being judged by a *group* rather than one individual. If it is preliminary hearing, a judge will make that decision, so it's the same song, third or fourth verse.

All right, the worst has happened—you've been bound over for trial. We'll assume bond has been continued, and your attorney fees are starting to make the national debt look like pocket change. At the trial, for the first time, you are about to be judged as to guilt or innocence by a jury of your peers. But are they really your peers? They are your equals in the eyes of God and (perhaps) the law, but have they had the same experiences and formed the same conclusions about life that you have? Have they ever been attacked by a raging maniac with two knives? Have they ever experienced violence at all? If they have, the prosecutor will have done everything possible to keep them off the jury. Your attorney should have done everything he could to get them on. If they are like the vast majority of people, they will never have experienced a truly violent attack themselves. They will have stumbled through life saying that they know such things occur but subconsciously believing they only happen in movies, on television, and in the newspapers. They may have a real problem understanding the reality of what you were forced to do. And the good Lord help you if they've bought into any of the "put an aura of goodness and light around you and you can't be harmed" pseudo-self-defense programs we've already discussed.

The bottom line is that all the men and women on your jury will be unique individuals. Like the cop who arrested you, the detective who conducted the interrogation, the assistant DA who decided to prosecute, and the judge who bound you over, they will have their own preconceived ideas about self-defense. This may work for you or against you. But this is why both your attorney and his opponent spent so much time picking them—both were trying to stack the deck in their favor.

No, it is not a perfect system we have. And in order to defend yourself *after* you have defended yourself, you must have at least a working knowledge of the flaws that exist within that system. You've got to guard against them, and if you can, use them to your advantage. If the idea of using the loopholes in the law bothers you morally, I can understand that. But rest assured that those trying to send you to the lethal-injection gallows for exercising your right to defend yourself will be trying to slip as much through the cracks in the structure as they can, too. That's what lawyers do for a living.

Let's go back to our hypothetical scenario and look at some other things of which you should be aware. We'll use a different example this time. An armed man threatens you with a gun, and you have no reasonable alternative to pumping a pair of .357 magnum hollow-points into his chest. First you should be certain, absolutely certain, that the attacker is indeed no longer a threat to you. Then it's time to call the cops.

Or is it? We are definitely working on one of those "Olympic rings" now, in which morality and legality may, or may not, overlap. Let me tell you this, however: 99.9 percent of the time, if you know you have acted reasonably in your own defense, you should report the incident. If this encounter occurred in your home, go ahead and get rid of the body if you'd rather, and spend the next two days scrubbing the blood out of the walls and carpet. Do all you can think of to get rid of everything that links you to the shooting. Police forensic experts will still find more than enough trace evidence to convict you if you come under suspicion. Successfully disposing of dead bodies and cleaning a scene of other physical evidence are tasks that require professionals—and they don't always do it right, either. And keep in mind that the moment you begin any kind of cover-up, each new step you take will likely become a step toward the penitentiary. The law and people in general still consider anyone who tries to hide his actions a criminal, and such actions can turn what might have been an open-and-shut case of justifiable homicide into a murder charge. Even if you are lucky enough to convince the jury that you panicked (or made the decision to cover your tracks for whatever other reason you made it) and that the two incidents—the shooting and the cover-up—are separate, you still have serious problems. You might walk on the murder charge, but you can still be charged with obstruction of justice.

All that said, I will admit there have been a few times when I did not heed my own advice. Instead of reporting a self-defense incident, I walked (or rather ran) away. I'm going to cite a couple as examples. In the first one, I think I made a bad decision in not waiting for the police to arrive. In the second, I believe I did the only reasonable thing I could do under the circumstances. I'm sure you will understand if I don't give all of the details.

The first incident involved a young man I would guess was about 15 years my junior (I had just celebrated my 40th birthday two days earlier). He was drunk and decided it would be fun to pick on me. He insulted me, and kept insulting me, until I finally found myself returning the insults, and returning them in far more creative ways than he was delivering them. This soon had his friends laughing at him instead of me, and this did not sit well with him. Actually, I was starting to have a pretty good time in this duel of wits with an unarmed man. But then he hit one of my sensitive buttons—he called me an "old man." (Remember that birthday, one of those traumatic ones with a zero on the end.) So I upped the ante by making a comment about his mother's profession, and suggesting that I might indeed be *his* "old man."

He took a punch at my face, and I had just enough time to move so that his fist struck the hard skull area just at my hairline (okay,

okay, just below my "old man" hairline). I believe he probably broke his hand. At least he was making the kind of noises we associate with such pain even before I stood up and started hitting him. Now, I didn't do any serious damage to the "kid," and perhaps he even learned a valuable lesson about wrinkled faces and receding hairlines that might save him worse injuries in the future. In any case, I decided that discretion might be the better part of valor, left the establishment, and passed the arriving patrol car (red lights and siren in full gear) as I drove away. I have not looked back since. Or been back, either. The next morning I also got a haircut and shaved my mustache.

Do you see the problems involved, though, even in a fairly minor incident like this? Did I worry about it? Of course I did. Every time the doorbell rang for the next two months I looked through the curtains to see if whoever was there had a warrant in his hand. There was a whole crowd of people who watched this silly little melodrama go down, and even though it was a place I had rarely gone before, there could have been someone there who knew me. Or someone could have gotten my license tag as I drove away. Again, or . . . or . . . or . . . or. Looking back on it now, I would have been better off waiting for the police and telling my story. I had not gone beyond reasonable force, but in our society flight is directly associated with guilt.

In the second situation, I'm afraid I'm going to have to be even more vague. I will say this, and it's the truth—it did not take place in the United States. I was attacked by two men on a dark and deserted side street, in an area of the city that only a fool or someone who had consumed far too much of the local wine would have stumbled into at that time of night. I'll let you guess which description applied to me: a) fool, b) drunk, or c) both of the above. In any case, I was there. This time, more serious physical damage occurred to my attackers, and I am convinced that I would have died that night if it hadn't. Did I report this incident to the police? No, I did not. I did not speak the language of the country. I had seen the movie *Midnight Express*. I got on the next train out of there and didn't get off again until I was two countries away. Good-bye and God bless. I didn't like my odds; those Olympic emblem rings just weren't overlapping enough to suit me. I have no problem living with my actions that night, either during or after the attack. I still think running like the wind was the right thing to do under the circumstances.

But let me stress again, not reporting a justified act of self-defense should be the exception rather than the rule. It should be considered only under the most extreme and unusual conditions. I could have been caught, and running would have made me look guilty of a crime even though I had not committed one. And saying I have no problem living with my actions is not precisely true. No, I don't have any problem with what I did from a moral standpoint. But legally? All I can say about that is that in writing about this event twenty-some years later, however vaguely, I'm still wondering if it wouldn't be wiser to just sweep the cursor across the whole section and then hit the delete button.

Let's look at how to handle a few specific problems that can arise in the aftermath of a self-defense situation. Again, it's impossible to cover every possibility and every potential variation of those possibilities. So even when I use a specific example, remember that I'm actually trying to convey to you more general concepts, which can be applied to your singular cases. Don't look at this as step-by-step directions.

A man breaks into your house. You reasonably believe he intends to kill you, or at least do you serious bodily harm. You shoot him, stab him, beat him with a piece of firewood (an old football buddy of mine did that to an intruder one time), or whatever. Now, during your call to the police you give the dispatcher only the bare facts, such as, "An armed man broke into my house, threatened me with a gun, and I was forced to shoot him." Remember to give a good description of your attacker as well as a good description of yourself and any family members or other people who are in the house legitimately. Then, if these descriptions and facts haven't been scrambled to the point of incoherence while being radioed to the patrol officers, there's at least some chance they won't shoot you by mistake when they arrive. Have a picture ID with your address on it ready if at all possible, as wounded assailants have been known to swear that they are in *their* house and that *you* broke in and attacked *them*. (This deception is discovered eventually, of course, but lots of bad things can happen before it is.)

Holding an intruder at bay while dialing the police is a dangerous time when attention is split between the immediate threat of violence and saying the wrong thing on the phone. This woman must be ready to fire at a moment's notice and at the same time be careful what she says to the dispatcher.

For everybody's sake, do not have a weapon of any sort in your hand when the cops come through the door. Right now, reading this, you probably realize that it isn't very smart without my telling you. But under the stress of having just defended their lives, and perhaps having had to take another, people have a tendency to cling to their weapons like Linus does his blanket. I mean, the thing in your hand just saved your life, right? The last thing you want to do is let go of it. With all that racing through your mind, and your blood pumping a million gallons a second, it's easy to forget how the police, who will be worried about getting killed themselves when they arrive, may react to the sight of a weapon in your hand.

So what should you do with your weapon? If your assailant is still alive, this can get tricky. Some people will tell you to keep the gun in your hand, then lay it down when you open the door. This could, of course, be the exact moment your live-but-subdued attacker makes his last-ditch attempt at escape, or killing you, or both. "Dead" bodies have also been known to be resurrected about this time and grab for the nearest gun. A far better solution, in my opinion, is to slip the weapon down the back of your pants just before you open the door. Then, with your empty hands in front of you in full view, immediately inform the officers that you are the homeowner, and that your weapon is in your belt behind you. Allow them to take it from you, and do not be surprised or offended if you find yourself on the floor in handcuffs until they feel that the scene is secured.

What do you tell the cops now? The oft quoted, "Don't say anything until you have your attorney present" is good advice. But it's easier to say than to actually put into practice. Actually, it's pretty easy for habitual criminals, but as Mr. Good Guy Honest Citizen you've always been taught to cooperate with the police, right? (Child: "Who's that man in blue, Mommy?" Mother: "That's a policeman, darling; he's your friend.") So your natural desire is going to be to cooperate, tell the responding officers what happened, and make sure they understand you really are the good guy. Your instincts will want this done as soon as possible. To follow those instincts in this case, however, is a mistake.

First of all, remember that you are under tremendous stress. During such times people quite often do not always express themselves correctly. They say things that can be misinterpreted, and sometimes they even say the exact opposite of what they mean. The responding officer's job is to record your words as close to verbatim as possible. So if you calmly say, "The man broke in, pointed a gun at me, and I was forced to shoot him," that is what will be entered into his report. Likewise, if you are still flowing with adrenaline, give out a loud war whoop, and then scream, "I woke up and found him in the living room and shot the son-of-a-bitch, and I'm glad he's dead!" that too will be entered exactly as you said it. Both statements convey essentially the same message but they do so in very different ways. The way you say things may affect the officer's attitude toward you and enter into his decision as to exactly what steps he should take next. The truth is, you probably are glad your attacker is dead because it means *you aren't*. But you do not need to say it. A cop who is a warrior and has experienced violence himself may understand your feelings. But remember that not all cops are warriors, and just because a man or woman wears a uniform does not mean he or she has ever faced life-threatening situations. Some police officers spend their entire cowardly careers making sure they're always safe and other officers take the risks.

Even if the responding officers understand the stress you are under, they must record your words exactly as you say them, and someone down the line in our system of "judges and juries" may not understand. Or they may choose to misinterpret your statements intentionally for their own self-serving reasons. In any case, the general public expects remorse on your part even when you had no other choice but to defend yourself.

My advice? Even if you are thrilled to death that you killed the evil miscreant, don't act like it.

Again, remember that the officer in charge at the scene is on the judge's seat for the moment, and to a certain extent your future rests in his hands. Refusal to speak at all, and demanding an attorney in an argumentative way, can turn a cop who might have been sympathetic to your predicament into a guy who doesn't like you very much. Rather than clamming up completely, repeat the same basic story that you told the dispatcher when you called 911 (it's already on record anyway). Then say something along the line of, "Officer, I'll be more than happy to cooperate and give you all the details a soon as I can. But right now I'm upset, and due to the seriousness of the matter, I really think I should consult my attorney first."

Such a statement is polite and respectful. Any reasonable police officer should understand it, and while I've already admitted that law enforcement has its share of jerks, most officers are reasonable. If you happen to get one of the jerks, he'll just have to dislike it; there's not a lot more you can do. If he tells you that if you don't come clean right now you're going to jail, go to jail. Believe me, considering the trauma you've just experienced, there is a high probability that you will say something that will someday come back to haunt you criminally, civilly, or both. No, jails are not pleasant places. But a little discomfort at this point can save you far more serious problems down the road.

One last thing before we move on. Do not do anything to alter the scene before the police arrive. *Please* do not believe the fools who tell you that if you shot the guy on your porch you'd better drag him inside. If you were justified in your actions, it makes no difference whether it was in your house, on your front porch, in your backyard, or anywhere else. Trying to alter the scene in your favor is similar to trying to get rid of the body, clean up your house, and act as if nothing happened; it is very easy for forensic specialists to determine that you did this, and it ruins your credibility from that point on.

So far, we've been talking primarily about life-and-death situations. But what about encounters like simple assaults? Let's say you're at a Little League game, and you and the father of an opposing team member exchange a few heated words. You think it's over, but after the game you find him waiting for you in the parking lot, and he throws a swing. You counter, a short fight ensues, and then it's over. What do you do?

Forget the after-game pizza long enough to drive immediately to the nearest police station. Ask for an officer, and tell him you need to make a report. Explain what happened, how you were forced to defend yourself, and how you used only the force necessary to stop the threat. (Okay, personally I don't care if you hit the creep a couple of extra times because he deserved it. But that should *not* be what goes into the report.) Be sure to give the officer the names of any witnesses, and be sure to point out any of them you know to be friends of the jerk. (They will have a completely different story from yours, believe me.) The officer taking your statement is going to ask you if you want to press charges. That's up to you. The important thing is that you got your story in first, and now if he comes along with his, it's your word against his. (Discounting possible witnesses.)

As long as no one was seriously injured, this is going to be a very low-priority case. Except in the smallest Podunkvilles where nothing else ever happens, the police won't have time to investigate further, and most DA's offices won't waste their time on it either. Of course, there are exceptions to this rule, and prosecution is always a possibility. Was the guy who swung at you the mayor? Did another father, an off-duty cop, see you throw your extra punches for good measure? Maybe. But in any case, you have now reported the incident and done about all you can do to protect yourself legally.

When you need an attorney, you need a good one. (I know "good attorney" is an oxymoron—I should have said *resourceful* instead of good.) In small- to medium-sized cities, where most of the judges and lawyers know each other, play golf together, and cheat on their wives at the same motel, you'd be wise to get a mouthpiece who is one of the "insiders." Chances are, your case will be decided over lunch or as one of them sinks a putt on the 14th hole. I would not recommend pulling in a big-city attorney, no matter how good he is. This creates hard feelings amongst the locals. Now, if your attorney decides to seek help from the same out-of-towner, that's another story. The local "clique" may not like it, but they will accept it. Calling F. Lee Bailey or Johnny Cochrane to represent you in a Midwestern city of 40,000 people, however, will have the judge and DA wanting to kill you before the trial even starts.

If you can't afford an attorney, one will be appointed for you. (Where'd I hear that?) Good luck. Public defenders are often attorneys who just passed the bar exam and didn't have good connections into a law firm. While there are, as always, exceptions to this rule, more than likely your counsel will have little experience. Or there will be other reasons he's getting paid a lousy salary for doing the same things other lawyers do and get rich. (Think about that.) He will also be carrying an extremely heavy caseload, so he may push you toward a plea bargain you do not want to accept. Or your case simply may not receive the attention it needs.

If you possibly can, you should hire your own attorney. Attorneys have been condemned since the profession began. Everyone from Jesus (read Luke XI: 46 and 52) to Shakespeare has had negative things to say about them, and most of them are true. But at this point, they are going to be a necessary evil, so get one who has a reputation for doing what he has to do to win. (Sound like self-defense in general?) You may even decide it's best to get the kind of lawyers O.J. Simpson had—did you see what they accomplished for him? Simpson's "dream team," as they were called, were a nightmare for justice. Attorneys like this simply stir up so much mud in the water that they confuse everyone from the judge on down. The result is total chaos. But look who's still riding around in his golf cart and talking about what a good football player he used to be.

Granted, assistant DAs are often in the same boat as inexperienced and overworked public defenders. Prosecuting does not pay nearly as well as defending, and for most it is just a stepping stone. But with a public defender the deck is stacked against you because the DA himself will be a well-seasoned attorney—and *politician*. He will be watching over major cases himself, or at least having one of his experienced staff do so. DAs do not like to lose because it costs them votes come reelection time.

Now, while you are out on bond awaiting trial, keep your mouth shut. Your attorney will tell you this, but I want to, too. And even if you win, keep your mouth shut *after* the trial as well. Do you remember Bernard Goetz? He legally and morally defended himself against three New York City subway punks, was charged with murder, and found not guilty. But Bernie just had to bask in the hero's limelight and rub the DA's nose in it. The result was that charges of possessing a firearm without a permit were filed, and this time he was convicted. He also lost a civil case for several million dollars. Not that the plaintiff will ever collect—old Bernie doesn't have it. But running your mouth off about a self-defense situation is never a wise thing to do.

Above all, under no circumstances should you talk to the press. I remember them from my own days as a cop, and I recall all too well their masterful ways of twisting things—and even blatantly lying when they need to do so for a better story. Recently, I watched a local television newscaster interview two people at the local boat club. The site had just been hit by a tornado, and the newswoman was covering the story live. She held her microphone out to the club's manager, who said, "We were lucky—it could have been a lot worse. We only had light damage to a few boats, and a few shingles blew off the roof."

Unsatisfied with this answer, the newswoman pushed the microphone past the manager to the "commodore" of the club. He made sure we knew his title first, then said, "We've had almost 250 boats damaged and extensive damage to the roof of the club house," pretty much contradicting the manager who still stood within the camera frame.

Which version do you think the newswoman went with? Right. But of course she had to add her own bit of sensationalism, too. Turning to the camera, she said, "Well, there you have it. Close to 300 boats ruined and the clubhouse totally destroyed."

I found this so remarkable (usually, the press is a lot sneakier and harder to catch doing these things) that I drove out to the boat club myself. As I suspected, the manager's assessment of the damage was far closer to the truth. But minor damage does not increase the sale of newspapers or help television ratings.

This story is demonstrative of how the press is willing to exaggerate details for a story. But it has nothing to do with self-defense or the law. So let's take a look at one a little "closer to home."

I have a close friend—a guy I go to the shooting range with—who works at another television station. Since at work he's surrounded by liberals who are totally ignorant of weapons, he's become the station's "gun expert." A few years ago, during a period of time when federal legislation to limit firearms' magazine capacity to 10 rounds was pending, one of the station's news writers came sprinting down the steps to his office. "Charlie, how many bullets does the clip of a .380 automatic hold?" she asked, huffing and puffing for breath. (We'll forgive her for calling a magazine a "clip." It was the least of her mistakes.)

"Well," Charlie said. "It depends on *what kind* of .380 you mean. Usually anywhere from seven to thirteen."

"I don't know what kind it was," the newswriter said.

"Then I can't tell you," was Charlie's reply.

The newswriter paused, then said, "But some of them can hold thirteen?"

Charlie, I'm sure, was thinking of the Beretta and Browning .380s with their double-stacked magazines when he said, "Well, a couple will take thirteen in the magazine and then you can chamber another."

"That's *fourteen?*" the newswriter asked. (I think a little applause for her mathematical mastery is in order here.)

"Well, yes but. . . ."

Charlie never got to finish his sentence because she turned on her heels and raced back up the steps. A few minutes later, the newscaster read a story about a .380 automatic being used in a robbery. He concluded with, ". . . experts say the gun may have held up to *fourteen* rounds!"

Don't tell me the media doesn't slant, spin, twist, and just flat outright lie when it fits its own selfish purposes. I've seen it happen too many times, both as a cop and as a civilian. You can't trust journalists any more than you'd trust that little sex-monkey Bill Clinton with your daughter. Just remember that a legitimate self-defense shooting doesn't sell newspapers or help TV ratings the way a murder does. Keep this in mind when the press wants to talk to you after you've defended yourself, and imagine how they can blow what you say out of proportion.

We've been assuming so far that you're being prosecuted unjustly for an act you committed in defense of yourself or a loved one. I've been a little pessimistic in my approach, but I've always followed the theory that you should hope for the best but prepare for the worst. In reality, far more cases of self-defense are not prosecuted than are. If you were forced to take a life to stay alive, there are two different ways the DA's office may handle it. The first is simply to decline to prosecute. This saves some hassles and attorney fees, but it means that charges could always be filed later somewhere down the line. I've still got one of those hanging over my head, and while it rarely crosses my mind anymore, I don't particularly like it when it does. There's always a chance, however slim, of some less-than-honorable DA or assistant seeing a way to gain notoriety by reopening an old case. To some it makes no difference whether you acted justly or not; if a conviction would help their careers, they'll go for it.

What is, in my opinion, a far better way to resolve the matter is for the DA to file it as justifiable homicide. When this is done, it means you are out of jeopardy at a future date. Just as you can't be tried twice for the same crime in this country, charges cannot be filed if a killing has been ruled a justifiable homicide.

Let's look at one last aspect of the law in relation to self-defense.

I hope there's no one out there so naive as to believe that the police can actually protect you. There's no group of men and women who would like to protect you more than the police, but it simply can't be done. The average self-defense situation lasts only a few seconds. The average response time for police to respond to an emergency is several minutes. You do the math. Attackers choose their times of attack when police aren't around. Hundreds of cases a day prove the police cannot arrive in time to help you. Several court rulings have stated that they aren't even expected to protect individual citizens, recognizing the futility of expecting them to do so. There is only one person who can protect you, and only one person who should be expected to do so: you. The police, your husband, your boyfriend, your wife, your father, or your brother may be the toughest SOBs in the valley, but they are not with you 24 hours a day, 365 days a year. The responsibility is yours, and yours alone.

Like so many other aspects of self-defense it is impossible to cover all the bases with regard to what might happen if you are prosecuted. In general, you should stay as calm as possible after an incident, notify the police, and get an attorney there with you at the scene if at all possible. He need not be the attorney you choose in the end to defend you if charges are filed, but somebody who has passed the bar exam should show up right away. That friend you play poker with twice a month who's a tax attorney or corporate lawyer will even do in a pinch, and he'll help you pick out a good criminal defense counselor if it comes to that. What you need even more than expert legal advice is a buffer who will stand between you and the police and keep reminding you to close your mouth every time you try to open it. Again, this is a time when emotions run high, and it's easy to make potentially incriminating statements even when you are completely innocent. Let things settle down. Speak privately with an attorney who understands the self-defense and lethal force statutes. Only then will you be able to give the police a clear, precise, and honest statement that cannot be misinterpreted later.

We have concentrated on the criminal justice system in this chapter, but the advice applies to civil law as well. While you will not go to prison if you lose a lawsuit, I am assuming you'd prefer not to lose everything you've worked for all your life either. Keep in mind that in a criminal case the prosecution must prove beyond a reasonable doubt that you committed a crime. To find you guilty in civil court, however, only a preponderance of evidence is required to show that you were at fault. Again, seek the advice of an attorney as soon as possible, and keep your mouth shut except when he advises you to speak.

While the laws are usually pretty clear, how they are interpreted almost never is. Much like clouds drifting over the courthouse, political climates come and go. The way self-defense is viewed today may change tomorrow and return again next week. Good luck. Make physical survival your top priority, but do all you can to make legal survival a close second.

New lords, new laws.

—John Harington
Nagae Antiquae, c. 1615

PART
2

FIGHT TIME

4

Martial Arts

A Realistic View

*He boxed, and he boxed with skill. His only problem was,
all the time he was boxing, I was hitting him.*
— Ernest Hemingway, describing a
boxing match he'd just had with a friend

By the time this book comes out it will have been more than 30 years since I first began the study of what we generally refer to as "traditional" martial arts. But it has been almost 20 years since I practiced them "according to Hoyle," and even longer than that since I was willing to blindly follow any system or teacher. The reason is simple: my primary interest is, and always has been, practical self-defense. And none of the "traditional" styles, be they Japanese, Chinese, Korean, or other, translate directly to actual close-quarters street combat as it exists today.

With very few exceptions, "traditional" martial arts in the United States give the student an unrealistic perspective on self-defense. Sometimes this is done deliberately—one of the many ways unscrupulous instructors have of sucking a pupil's wallet dry. Other times it is unintentional; the instructor himself has been the victim of too much unconfirmed hypothesis. But whether such false confidence is passed on unwittingly rather than dishonestly, the result is no less devastating when the student is someday called upon to defend life and limb.

There are many conflicts between realistic personal protection and "traditional" martial arts. One is the fact that the vast majority of "traditional" training today takes place under unrealistic conditions. It may be 100-degrees Fahrenheit on the sidewalk outside, but the student dons his gi in an air-conditioned dressing room and then steps out onto the mat in an equally climate-controlled dojo. He is barefoot or wearing lightweight footwear, and he has on a loose-fitting garment that is ideal for moving freely—not the restrictive jeans and heavy shoes he will put on when he leaves. As he goes about his workout, bowing and parroting phrases in a language he does not understand, paying homage to religions in which he does not believe, he is carefully observed by an instructor who makes sure he abides by the rules governing respect, courtesy, and safety.

Which brings us to the second major conflict between "traditional" martial arts and realistic self-defense: rules. In true self-defense, the only rule is that different levels of threat require different degrees of response, and this rule applies only to you. An attacker bent on doing you grave bodily harm has already thrown the rule book out the window and proven he is willing to violate the laws of society. Just how far outside those parameters is he willing to go? If you teach yourself to be observant and intuitive, you may be able to quickly read the rules by which he is playing (is he intent on killing you or does he just want to play "tough guy") and react accordingly. But you must always keep in mind that you may have misread his intent or that his original plan of "rob and run" or "scare and laugh" may suddenly escalate into a life-threatening encounter.

There are other problems when attempting to apply the "traditional" martial arts to practical self-defense today. Some systems favor kicking, others hand strikes. Some concentrate on sport, or artistic and spiritual perfection, while others teach glamorous and flashy movie techniques that even Chuck Norris, Steven Seagal, and John-Claude VanDamme (all accomplished martial artists as well as actors) would never attempt in a life-threatening situation. Many systems focus on standing combat and ignore the fact that many encounters end up on the ground. At the other extreme, devotees of the grappling arts profess their disciplines to be supreme by pointing to the fact that grapplers almost always take the title in the "no-holds-barred" Ultimate Fighting Championships (UFC). The Ultimate Fighting Championships supposedly reflect the reality of a street fight and are publicized as "anything goes" tournaments. Actually, while the UFC's rules permit a tremendous amount of brutality, it still has rules. The UFC does not permit biting, choking, eye gouging, and many other techniques that are viable in true self-defense. Furthermore, while it is true that many skirmishes do go to the ground, in many others, only the loser hits the canvas.

Current wisdom among the grapplers is that only a fighter trained in judo, jujitsu, wrestling, or a similar mat-based discipline stands a chance in a real fight. Tell that to Mohammed Ali, Evander Holifield, and Mike Tyson. (I'd advise doing so over the phone rather than in person.) And while effective grappling is a tremendous skill that can benefit anyone's overall self-defense package, it is not the end-all solution any more than any other art is. It can be disastrous when fighting an attacker armed with a knife, and rest assured that when you're attacked by multiple opponents, if you're rolling around with one guy, his friends will be kicking you in the back of the head.

With very few exceptions, what we call the "traditional" martial arts focus on specific aspects of fighting while neglecting others. They train their students, either consciously or unconsciously, to observe rules not applicable to street defense. Another of the major problems with the "traditional" systems is that they are so often taught by people who have never even been in a grade school playground fistfight. These instructors are usually very good, well-meaning human beings, but they came up the ranks, received their belts, and began teaching without ever having been forced to put their theories to the test.

Perhaps the best example I have ever seen of this came from my own nephew who is a brown belt at a dojo in the Dallas-Fort Worth area. During a recent visit, he proudly demonstrated to me how he had been taught to disarm someone holding a gun by executing a crescent kick and "knocking the gun from the guy's hand." His second method was this absolutely ridiculous "X-block" designed to "break the opponent's wrist." In the first case, hands move much faster than legs, and about the time his foot left the ground he'd get a bullet in the chest. In the second case, there is no guarantee that the gunman's wrist would be broken (particularly by an 11-year-old boy), and even if it were, such a break does not necessarily paralyze the trigger finger. It almost broke my heart to have to demonstrate to my nephew, who had worked so hard for and was so proud of the rank he now held, why neither technique was viable.

This is hardly an isolated case. Such erroneous instruction by unrealistic teachers is rampant these days. Normally, when I come across such things I try to be polite, and if the situation calls for it, I attempt to show the student the discrepancies in this "dojo thinking." In the case of my nephew, however, I'm tempted to drive down to Dallas and kick his instructor's butt myself. He's teaching a kid I love—and others like him—things that may well get him killed.

By now you're undoubtedly wondering why I keep putting the word "traditional" in quotes (and you may even be getting a little tired of it!). The short version is that the word "traditional" is just flat incorrect as we use it pertaining to martial arts.

The long version begins with the fact that the marital arts we refer to as "traditional," as they are taught in America today, are ancestral in technique only, not in spirit. They were originally developed as practical means of self-defense for a specific time and place. Each system incorporated the weapons available at the time; the specific geographical terrain of the area; and the size, strength, physical condition, and social outlook of the people who would utilize it. The techniques that evolved were those deemed best for those people of that time and in that place.

The word *evolved*, in fact, is the operative word that separates "traditional" systems from today's practical defense. In the days when the "traditional" systems were used in actual combat rather than merely practiced as arts, they were constantly evolving. When practical new techniques were discovered, they were incorporated into the program. If a technique proved useless in battle, it was discarded. As technology progressed and new weapons were developed, they too were added. It was not until these systems were no longer needed for "everyday" defense and began to be practiced as arts that they became static rather than active and evolutionary in nature.

There is a real beauty in the "traditional" arts, and I have great respect for those involved in them. But in most cases, this respect is often more akin to that which I have for great musicians, painters, or dancers than the respect I hold for great fighters. Go to a "traditional" martial arts school and you are likely to find some very tough black belts. They know the difference between the dojo and the street. You will, however, also find a good number of dreamers wearing black around their waists. They have no conception of what real violence entails and, in a serious confrontation without referees and rules, they stand little chance of emerging victorious against even an average street fighter.

Please do not misinterpret my words. Very good self-defense techniques can be gleaned from such arts as judo, karate, kung fu, and others. Aikido, for example, known as the most gentle of arts, can produce some of the toughest (yet temperate) fighters around when it is taught correctly by a good instructor who emphasizes the difference between dojo and street. But the key word is *gleaned*. Many, many black belt instructors today are not that good at teaching reality because they have not experienced it themselves. The serious student of practical combat must pick and choose which techniques are street-worthy in the America of the 21st century and discard those that were designed for 18th century China, Okinawa, Korea, or Japan. During this harvesting process, the student of combat will also be hampered by the tremendous amount of time "traditional" schools spend on the art and sport facets of martial arts. A typical 90-minute class may include as much as 30 minutes of exercise, 55 minutes of "art and sport" and, if the student of hand-to-hand combat is lucky, 5 minutes of serious defense work. Don't bother asking your instructor why he doesn't spend more time on self-defense; his answer will be that you are perfecting it through the art and sport.

Unfortunately, nothing could be further from the truth.

The "art" aspect of the martial arts is usually expressed in the attempt to perfect form, both in individual techniques (kicking, punching, and the like) and in the prearranged combinations of these techniques known as kata in Japanese and Okinawan arts (and by other terms, depending upon the country of the art's origin). While these dance-like exercises are indeed one way to practice fighting techniques, they are hardly the best way. Most kata, in fact, were originally designed to appear to be dances and thus disguise such forbidden training from the eyes of enemies occupying the region. In true self-defense, perfect form is not necessary; speed, accuracy, and sufficient power are what count. Executing the technique effectively is the important thing, not how pretty it looks.

The "sport" aspect of the martial arts today is often thought to be the best training for self-defense. In reality, it has some very damaging side effects for the participant who may someday fight for his life. Karate point-fighting preconditions the mind to pull punches and kicks and ignore vital striking areas that violate the rules of the game. These areas may be sorely needed when it is no longer a "game" and your life is suddenly on the line rather than the loss of a point or match. Even in full-contact competition, be it with protective equipment or bare-knuckled as in the Ultimate Fighting Championships, competitors must abide by rules that forbid certain techniques and striking areas. The competitive fighter runs a tremendous risk of becoming desensitized to reality and, again, entering one of those states of false confidence we have already discussed.

Let me relate a funny story that illustrates this. Many years ago my next door neighbor, who was a local judge and long-time friend, held a party to celebrate my 30th birthday. Some time during the evening, I left with him and another friend, an off-duty police officer, to make a beer run. (I tell you their professions simply because it adds to this story of three men in their 30s acting like idiots.) Driving along the main drag of our hometown—the same main drag we had haunted as teenagers—we were passed by a carload of young men who promptly gave us the finger.

Now, at this point we somehow passed though a time warp. We were supposed to be grown men, but suddenly we were all three shooting the bone right back at them and returning their adolescent threats with our own, equally childish, retorts. (I told you in the Introduction that some of these examples were going to be embarrassing.) It was the '60s all over again; at least 10 years had been subtracted from our ages, and a good deal more than that number of points from our IQs. Both cars pulled over to a park—the same park where we had settled similar disputes when our ages at least gave us some excuse for such juvenile behavior. We all got out of the cars, and the judge and I promptly began laughing our butts off as we neared the end of the time warp and suddenly realized just how ridiculous it all was. But our cop friend, who had been a little more responsible for the needed beer run than the others at the party, was still in the eye of the warp itself. He and a young man of around 20 years of age squared off.

Now began a fight, which confirmed something I had suspected for some time: too much free sparring (or free fighting) is bad for the soul. This kid was obviously well trained. He looked great. He was dancing and weaving, whirling, and jumping. Roundhouse and spinning back kicks were flashing beneath the streetlights. But none of these beautiful flashy techniques were landing on my cop friend.

I watched this young man closely. Was he just playing cat and mouse with my friend? I had once done that with a drunk who came into my dojo looking for trouble, humiliating him and allowing him to wear himself out without actually hurting him. But the kid actually appeared to be trying to strike his opponent. His eyes reflected determination. But on his face I also saw an ever-widening expression of disillusionment. Things just weren't quite "clicking" the way he'd been taught they would.

Later I learned that this young man was an excellent tournament fighter from another school. But he had trained so long and hard for point-fighting competition that now, finding himself in a real situation, he was still pulling his punches and kicks.

Sirens sounded in the distance, pushing the three of us who were experiencing an early "second childhood" on out the other end of the time warp and back into our car. We were gone by the time the responding officers arrived, and thus avoided an embarrassing situation in which the boys in blue would have had to decide whether or not to arrest a fellow officer, a judge, and a deputy sheriff.

No damage was done. Oh, I think our off-duty cop friend had a bloody nose—big deal. All in all, it was a silly-ass little encounter of no significance, and even though it took place on the street rather than in the dojo, certain unwritten rules were followed. The objective was to hurt the other person—but only to a degree. Neither the flashy young tournament man nor my off-duty cop friend wanted to kill or even seriously injure his opponent. In fact, the only real difference in the rules between the dojo and the street was that bare-knuckled contact was allowed. It was classic affective, rather than predatory, combat behavior.

Still, that night I learned a significant lesson on a much deeper level than I had understood it before. It is not a new idea; you have heard it over and over, but like me up until that evening, you may not have actually observed it firsthand. *You will fight the way you train.* And if you train incorrectly for street defense, you will fight incorrectly.

So if your only (or at least your primary) interest is self-defense, how should you train? As realistically as possible, of course. But that presents its own problems. Completely realistic training would mean all-out, hell-bent-for-leather combat. At least periodically, you and a training partner would have to fight to the death. The one who didn't die would end up in prison with far more realistic training partners than he wanted. Therefore, pragmatic practicing usually means breaking your program into parts, learning some of the realism from each piece, and then putting the pieces together in your mind.

For example, prearranged repetitive exercises such as Okinawan Goju-Ryu karate's many *bunkai* and *kiso-kumite*, or Filipino flow drills like *sumkete* and others can teach speed, timing, and technique. Two-man "surprise" reaction drills—not prearranged—develop response time. In these two training methods, practitioners will, like the tournament fighter, have to pull punches. But power of technique—and the "different feel" of striking a hard object rather than air or a cooperative partner—can be added to the equation by employing a heavy bag, focus mitts, striking posts, and other inanimate targets.

A good set of boxing gloves can teach the student to take blows without doing serious damage, and speed bags train timing and coordination. Double-end striking balls add yet another dimension to your program. Actual sparring, or free fighting, is fine as long as it is kept in perspective and not overdone. Otherwise, it is very likely to be confused with the "real thing" and, as we've already seen, that's dangerous. Had the young tournament champion we looked at earlier been fighting someone intent on hurting him, he very likely would have been injured.

When training for self-defense, keep in mind that every physical movement you make on this planet, be it during a fight, on the job, or while eating dinner, making love, or even sleeping, falls into 12 basic planes of motion commonly referred to as the 12 Angles of Attack. They are numbered differently by different groups who use this learning tool. But just as it's not essential to know the correct sequence of a kata (form) to understand the techniques, it doesn't matter if you know the right numbers because there aren't any right numbers—just numbers.

We'll assume you are right-handed. You lefties get the short end of the stick as usual, but most of you have learned to expect that over the years. (The fact is, you may learn this even better because it will force you to think for yourself like I've been preaching about doing.) If you look at your target area like a clock, number 1 is a movement from approximately 2:00 to 8:00. Number 2 starts at 10:00 and ends at 4:00. I'm going to skip to number 5 now, because now that you see the pattern you can figure out 3, 4, 9, 10, 11, and 12 simply by following the arrows on the chart.

As you see, the numbers I just named have arrows accompanying them. 5, 6, 7, and 8 do not. That is because we are looking straight ahead at a two-dimensional page, and these numbers are moving forward, into the third dimension we can't see. They represent thrusts with a knife or stick and straight punches or other strikes with the empty hand. Angle 5 is a straight forward thrust. Angle 6 is a palm-down thrust that angles in toward the oppenent's centerline. Angle 7 is a backhand version of Angle 6, delivered palm up and angling in toward the centerline. Finally, Angle 8 is a downward backhand strike that can be repeated to create a circular pattern on the left side of your body. Numbers 1 through 4 and 9 through 12 can also be performed as thrusts. But they can also be more circular slashes or chops with a weapon and open or close-fisted equivalents with the empty hand.

These movements, which are really just the rudimentary physics of body mechanics, hold true regardless of what weapon you use. They are, with very minor modifications, the same with a hand, foot, elbow, knee, knife, Filipino *baston*, baseball bat, claw hammer, screwdriver, Japanese *jo*, collapsible baton, police riot stick, Chinese

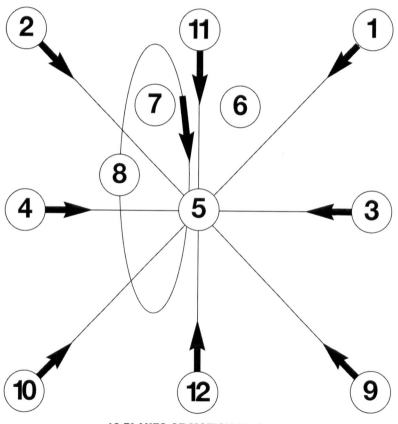

12 PLANES OF MOTION DIAGRAM

broadsword, cane, hiking staff, tomahawk, socket wrench, pliers, Italian flanged mace, office chair, computer mouse, jar of pickled herring, and every other object in the universe that might be used to cut, stab, or strike someone.

The basics are pretty elementary. But within each of these basic movements lies the potential for countless minor variances, and it is these little deviations within that fundamental simplicity, these minuscule changes that take a technique and make it uniquely yours—the ones you come up with on your own—that make your movements effective.

If you have been, or currently are, a formal student of the martial arts, think back on how many times you have learned a new drill that involved a partner, then practiced it with that partner, over and over, until you'd memorized it. Then, the instructor spoke those words you knew were coming and had been unconsciously dreading: "Very good. Now change partners." A new face and a new body suddenly stood before you. The brain behind that face, and the body below it, had learned the same drill you had only moments before, and theoretically you both should have been able to take up the drill once more without breaking stride. But that didn't happen, did it? No, the same drill was different now. Not a lot—just enough to throw you off. This new person across from you didn't move with exactly the same timing as your earlier partner had, he didn't look the same, and more importantly to experienced fighters, he didn't "feel" the same. The subtleties involved here are more easily recognized by advanced students, since the other mistakes beginners make often overshadow this phenomenon and allow it to go unnoticed. (In other words, it's still there, but there are other problems, even more important, that must be overcome first.) This is why, in actual combat, although you may have practiced defending against a specific technique thousands of times over, when a new attacker throws it, his way of doing so is different enough that he's able to bust it through your defenses.

Back to the chart for a minute. In your mind, superimpose it over the face of an imaginary opponent. Now drop it to his chest, now to his groin. These are the high, mid, and low lines of attack (*jo, chu,* and *gei* to you hardcore Japanese traditionalists), and each attack—thrust or punch, slash or chop—may be delivered at any of the lines. They may also be delivered with a full, follow-through motion or a short, snapping action that retracts from the target after striking. The Filipino arts call the follow-through *lobtik* and the retracting strike *witik*. It's sort of the difference between a car that runs over you and drives on and one that hits you, backs up, and prepares to ram you again.

You karate, tae kwon do, kung fu, and other guys—let's drop this to your level so you can understand. (Just kidding—smile a little between *kiais*, okay?) Looking at the chart, if you deliver a straight reverse punch to the sternum, along which line are you moving? Number 5. How about a front snap kick to the groin? If you said 12, go to the head of the class. A hammerfist that starts directly overhead and moves straight down? Did you say 11? You win the prize. A right-handed backfist that begins roughly at your left shoulder and moves to the nose of an opponent facing you? Number 8? Ah, Grasshopper! You are ready to leave the temple!

Your biggest problem in putting all this into perspective will probably come (mine did) from the fact that it is so simple. Once you understand these 12 angles of attack there is absolutely nothing mysterious about them, so for some people it's like an adult trying to understand a child's riddle—we're looking for a hidden, complex answer when the correct one is right there before our very eyes. So as we continue to get more specific in the next few chapters, remember: look at the forest, not the trees.

My recommendations on training in this chapter focused primarily on unarmed combat, but the approach to training with hand-held nonprojectile weapons is almost the same, and even firearms training must be broken into parts. We'll cover this more extensively in the appropriate chapters.

For years now, we Americans have had a love affair with the Asian arts. This would have been fine had we not carried it to the point of absurdity, deifying Asian fighting techniques and the philosophies behind them, and interpreting both as almost supernatural. In reality, much of the Zen-riddle aspect of the philosophy that intrigues us so is merely common sense reflected through the

Eastern rather than the Western mind. The Oriental mind has developed a little differently than its Occidental counterpart throughout history. Its view of—and approach to—life differs slightly. I am not saying it is better or worse, just different. However, it is not as different as some would have you believe. In my experience, it is just different enough to happily confound Westerners who love the inexplicable so much that they insist on being confounded even at this "fortune cookie" depth.

This rather childish, fad-like obsession with Oriental philosophy is equally present when we view the Asian fighting techniques themselves. They are no better—and some would argue that they are worse—than the combat systems that have developed in the Western world. But we all love the mysterious. So we catch an old Bruce Lee movie on cable TV, see him leap 20 feet into the air or kick a thrown knife back into the chest of the man who threw it, and a secret little part of us wants to believe these things could be done. Well, maybe *that* couldn't really be done, we grudgingly admit to ourselves. But Bruce knew . . . well, *secrets.*

Ladies and gentlemen, Bruce Lee was a very fine martial artist, perhaps, as some say, the best, but even he could not do off screen what he did on. However, he did know one secret that seems to have passed over the heads of a lot of people in today's society. He knew that if he took the natural talent God gave him and then worked his butt off to develop it, he would become good. Now that you know the secret, you can do the same. It is not restricted to self-defense; rather it applies to all areas of life, and it's the only "secret of life" I've ever come across that ever worked.

As already touched upon, America's obsession with the Asian martial arts has led to an ignorance of our own fighting systems. I find it curious that while most American martial artists today readily recognize the name Miyamoto Musashi, mention of the equally great British swordsman George Silver usually brings blank stares. The Asian arts have been in America for a long time now—long enough for anyone interested to be exposed to them. So are they really superior to the fighting systems developed in Europe and America? If so, why have boxers not replaced jabs and hooks with the punches of karate and tae kwon do? Why, in kickboxing, was it necessary to incorporate a rule requiring a minimum number of kicks per round? And why do the contestants usually throw their mandatory kicks half-heartedly, expending as little energy as possible, then knuckle down to serious boxing again? Are the Japanese tanto and the system developed around it really better than the bowie knife and its system of modified saber fencing? Are the Japanese *katana* and Filipino *barong* better swords than the Scottish claymore or the Roman gladius?

Recently I was honored to help referee Hock Hochheim's Congress of American Knife Fighters "Kill Shot" contest. About 50 contestants took part in what is basically knife sparring with rubber knives and pads. It can, and does, get vicious sometimes. Competitors came from a wide variety of styles—Japanese, Chinese, Korean, Filipino, Thai, and all the others. But the man who won—and won handily, I might add—was a drama professor who studied fencing and had a very limited background in the Eastern arts. Food for thought.

Every "traditional" fighting system, East or West, has its strong and weak areas, and none is tailor-made for any one individual. The wise warrior knows this and acts accordingly, studying a variety of styles and taking what works for him from each. This is, indeed, what Bruce Lee was in the process of doing with jeet kune do at the time of his death.

In the last few years there has been a new wave of martial arts in the United States that stresses true combat over art and sport, fighting over system. Still in its infant stage, it is nevertheless growing rapidly. This new wave of thinking recognizes that the vast majority of men and women who enter a dojo do so with the serious goal of learning to defend themselves—not to win trophies or take up a new hobby. It also understands that most people today are far too busy to reap the wheat from the chaff, and therefore wastes no time on formalities and other nonessential ceremonies. Some "traditionalists" have claimed that this direct approach robs the student of the proper "morality" that should accompany such teaching. Nonsense. A moral sense of right and wrong can easily be instilled without turning class-

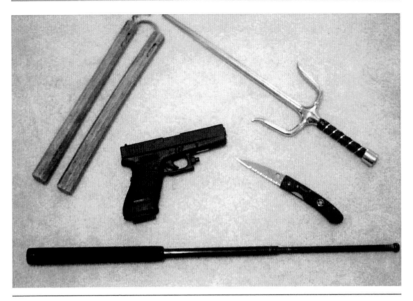

Then and now. The weapons of yesteryear were fine for their time. Today, they look out of place and there are far better alternatives. Top: Okinawan nunchuku and sai. Middle: Glock 21 .45-caliber automatic pistol with Aero-Tek 2010 laser sight; Spyderco Centofante II folding knife. Bottom: ASP collapsible baton.

es into rituals of foreign religions to which the student does not even acquiesce. In the new systems morality and legality are taught with a direct American, rather than a roundabout Oriental, approach, which far better suits the mentality. And beyond morality, legality, and the warrior mind-set, philosophy is not taught in addition to technique. As my old friend Korean Master Jack Hwang once said, "You want to learn to fight? Stay here. You want to pray? Go to church."

While nontraditional in the sense that it is a new approach in the United States, this new American method is traditional in that it is in keeping with the spirit of the martial arts. Just as traditional martial artists did before their styles of fighting became art and sport, the new American warrior takes advantage of the technology of today, incorporating firearms, lock-blade folding knives, and other weapons of our time into his training. Students are not as likely to be found practicing with nunchuku, bo, and sai as they are pocketknife, claw hammer, and screwdriver—the tools and weapons of our modern society.

We're about to move on into the chapters on specific means of defense. As we do, I hope you will keep these observations I have made over the last 30 years in mind. And here's something else to think about as you read on. In Chapter 1 I gave you a faulty formula held by some people regarding courage: Danger + Fear = Cowardice. Well, here's a formula you can take to the bank:

1 determined 12-year-old + 1 sharp pocketknife = 12 years in a gi.

There is nothing in words. Believe what is before your eyes.

—Ovid
Fasti, II, c. 5

5

Firearms

The Ultimate in Personal Self-Defense

You ask me if a man may become sufficiently skilled in the martial arts to empty-handedly defeat an opponent with a gun? My answer is, "Yes, of course this is possible. But in addition to skill, the martial artist must be very lucky. And the man with the gun must be very stupid."

—Sekeichi Toguchi
Grandmaster of Okinawan
Karate-do Goju-Ryu Shoreikan
December 15, 1972

Unlike most of the quotations I have chosen for this book, I heard these words spoken in person. I had spent several weeks studying directly under Mr. Toguchi, and was surprised that my actual black belt exam lasted only around 45 minutes. At the celebration afterwards, I sat on the floor with other karateka, eating and drinking and laughing, wearing my brand new stiff-as-a-board first-degree black belt, while the grandmaster answered questions through his interpreter. Mine had been about the short duration of the test, to which Mr. Toguchi had laughed and said, "Tonight was a mere formality. I've been testing you for weeks."

But it was a green belt, whose name I'm afraid is long forgotten to me, who asked the question so pertinent to this chapter. How well I recall the smiling Toguchi-sensei—who had been one of the great Chojun Miyagi's five original students—as the words were translat-

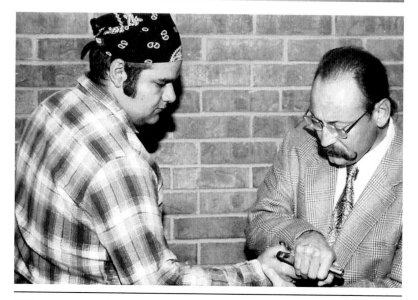

Taking a gun away from an attacker is risky business but can be done with enough practice and confidence. Perhaps the most important aspect is that once committed, you must follow through. Hesitation means death.

ed to him. It was obvious he'd been asked the same question many times in the past because even though he spoke to his interpreter in Japanese, I could tell the words were well rehearsed.

My good friend Master at Arms Jim Keating has another way of putting it: "On the streets, weapons rule. You don't hear about too many drive-by kickings."

And so goes the world.

No one weapon is perfect for every self-defense situation. But in today's society, there is nothing as effective overall as the firearm. The old saying, "God made men but Sam Colt made them equal," is even more relevant in the 21st century than it was in the 19th century of Colonel Colt. Technology has created handguns far beyond old Sam's wildest dreams, with lightweight polymer construction that stands up to the recoil trauma caused by high-caliber rounds; shotguns that will hold up to 10 or more shells of 00 buckshot; rifles that can put 5 rounds into the same hole at 400 yards; and full-auto sub-

In today's world, competence in unarmed self-defense is not enough. The only chance the young man on the sidewalk has is to return fire.

machine guns that can empty a 30-round magazine before the inexperienced shooter can let up on the trigger. Firearms have the advantage of being useful at a variety of ranges, from point-blank contact shots all the way out to however far the particular gun you are firing will carry the particular cartridge with which it was chambered.

But like any other weapon, guns also have some disadvantages. We'll cover them partially in this chapter and even more when we compare guns to knives and sticks and other weapons.

For the purposes of this book, we're going to look primarily at the handgun, since this is most often the first line of defense for both civilians and police officers. Soldiers usually rely on rifles or submachine guns as their primary weapon, while the pistol, if carried at all, is relegated to the role of "backup." But before we get into handguns, let's at least take a general look at these other weapons as they relate to personal defense in today's society.

If I lived in a rural area, I would most definitely keep a good rifle

This photo depicting a "drive-by kicking" pretty much speaks for itself, don't you think?

or carbine (for the uninformed, a carbine is a somewhat shorter rifle chambered to fire handgun rounds) loaded and ready to defend myself and my family. Nothing stops an attacker faster than a good .308 or similar round traveling at thousands of feet per second. Nothing, however, travels as far in a direction you didn't want it to go if you miss your target or, like the Energizer Bunny, just keeps on going through a target of flesh-and-bones that you do hit. In the country, you have a fairly wide margin for such errors. In the city you do not. Rifles, because of their size, are difficult to conceal, heavy to carry, and hard to maneuver in confined spaces.

While shotguns are perhaps the safest of all firearms as far as missed shots and overpenetration of a target are concerned (no guns are perfectly safe in this respect) and will stop even the most determined aggressor with a couple of 12-gauge loads to center of mass, they are similar to rifles in that they are difficult to conceal, carry, and maneuver. If you have taken advantage of the new "shall issue" concealed-carry permits now available in many states (and I hope you have), remember that your new little permit card means exactly what is says—your weapon must remain concealed except when in use. Unless you are willing to wear a trench coat 365 days a year and be mistaken for a bank robber, the shotgun doesn't fit the profile. They are also big, heavy and, again like the rifle, harder to carry even when not concealed. This is why you usually see police shotguns locked in vehicle racks rather than slung over the officer's shoulder. When you're inside a house, moving down a narrow hallway, turning blind corners, and moving up or down stairs, they are also less maneuverable. While both shotguns and rifles can be fired quite accurately within typical self-defense range with only one hand, they were designed as two-handed weapons and cannot be utilized as effectively with only one. Self-defense often dictates that the "off" or "weak" hand (the one not carrying the primary weapon) is called upon to perform a variety of support tasks, such as opening doors, turning on lights, holding a flashlight, or even defending from a sudden, unanticipated attack that got between you and the long barrel of your weapon. The shotgun can be quite clumsy under such conditions.

For the vast majority of people, submachine guns are impractical for self-defense. Oh, they're great fun to shoot, and in military and certain police operations they are the ideal weapon. But for the city or rural homeowner, they rarely (notice I never say never?) fit the bill. It is not, as is commonly believed, illegal to own fully automatic weapons in every state. In my home state of Oklahoma, a full-auto rifle or submachine gun may be purchased legally from an authorized dealer after an application has been submitted and the appropriate tax stamp issued by the Bureau of Alcohol, Tobacco, and Firearms (BATF). But even though it's legal, let me tell you what will happen if you use it to defend yourself.

In general, you'll double the problems that you face in the aftermath of a shooting, and take it from me, the paperwork and other hassles involved even after using a "kinder, gentler" weapon are bad enough. The use of a fully automatic weapon may, in and of itself, be the factor that tips the scale against you when the DA decides whether to prosecute or not. Your assailant will not be any more dead than if you had defended yourself with a Colt Single Action Army "cowboy gun" with Roy Rogers' picture and "Happy Trails" engraved on the frame, but the entire incident will be viewed differently. This is not very intelligent thinking, and it is not right. But nobody ever accused attorneys of doing what was right—just doing what it takes to win. Yes, it is stupid to assign human characteristics like "good or evil" to inanimate objects, but some people do. They view certain weapons as possessing varying degrees of social acceptability while others are seen as inherently evil. You may be sure that if you do end up in court, no matter how justified your actions, you will hear the phrases "full automatic!" and "assault weapon!" and "not meant for anything but killing people!" over, and over, and over. References to Al Capone, John Dillinger, and whatever murderers are currently in the headlines that week will fall over the courtroom like so much excrement from a flock of overflying geese.

While there are experts who disagree with me, I personally choose the handgun over any other firearm for personal defense, both on the streets and at home. Even the largest pistols and revolvers may be concealed by the average person if need be, and concealing the small- to medium-frame weapons can be done quite easily and comfortably. Handguns can be maneuvered sufficiently with one hand. So it will be the pistol and revolver we look at most closely in the rest of this chapter, but as we do, keep in mind several things. No two self-defense situations are exactly the same, and therefore no one firearm is ideal under all circumstances. No two human beings have the same exact life-styles and because of this each individual's specific self-defense needs are a little different from anyone else's. So if you decide that a rifle, shotgun, carbine, or even a weapon capable of full-auto fire better fits your requirements, then by all means go that route. As I tried to stress in the last chapter, I am your guide, not your guru. I am attempting to assist you in thinking for yourself in terms of defense, not to create a following of mindless robots who shout out, "*Hai*, Sensei!" or "Yes, Master!" at my proclamations. (If you knew me, you wouldn't even be tempted.)

CHOOSING A HANDGUN

First, let's look at how to decide what handgun is right for you. There are a few general guidelines I follow, and would like to pass them on: 1) You should use the largest caliber you can accurately control up through .45 ACP in semiautomatics and .44 Special in revolvers. Beyond those calibers—.44 magnum, .50 AE, and the like—the law of diminishing returns comes into play, and much of the bullet's energy passes through the human body without taking effect. Except in cases where certain physical disabilities or other unique circumstances are factors, calibers should never be smaller than .380 (9mm *Kurz* or Short) automatic or .38 Special in the "wheel guns." At the same time, keep in mind that a .22 in the hand is worth two .44 magnums "in the bush." 2) You should make a realistic assessment concerning how much, and how often, you will train. The amount of practice you engage in has a direct relationship on more than marksmanship; it breeds familiarity with the weapon. And the more complex the weapon's function, the more familiarity is required. For the vast majority of people interested only in self-defense, the KISS principle applies: Keep It Simple, Stupid. This usually means that the best choice is a revolver, or at least a double-action or what is commonly referred to as a double-action-only (which in reality is a single-action but let's not get confused at this point!) automatic. (We also say *automatic* when what we really mean is *semiautomatic*—one pull of the trigger delivers one shot.) 3) You must accurately define the role your defense firearm will play. Will it be kept at home, with home defense its only purpose, or will it be carried? If it's the latter, will you tote it daily or only on specific occasions? Will you carry it in your car or on your person?

With these things in mind, let's look at what kinds of guns there are to choose from these days. Semiautos (and from now on, since I've explained the discrepancy in terms, I'm just going to go with the flow and call them autos) have been around since the late 1800s. But because of their more complex mechanical function, it took years to perfect them to the point of acceptable reliability. As late as the 1970s, the majority of even the best automatic pistols were extremely sensitive to certain loads and bullet shapes. My Browning Hi-Power 9mm, which I purchased in 1973, worked flawlessly with full-metal jacket bullets—perhaps the absolute worst round ever invented for self-defense purposes. It also fed hollow-points that closely

There is a wide variety of handguns available today that are suitable for self-defense. Top, left to right: Glock 27 .40-caliber pistol (Mini-Glock), Smith & Wesson 642 .357 Magnum with Barami Hip-Grip and Mel Tyler T-Grip, Taurus Model 44 .44 Magnum, Browning .40-caliber Hi-Power. Below: American Derringer DA38 in .40 caliber, Ruger Vaquero in .45 Colt. (Although the single-action revolver would not be the first choice for a defense gun, it will definitely throw the bullet out of the barrel just like the others.)

resembled the full-metal jackets in shape—rounds that were meant to expand upon contact and sometimes did and sometimes didn't. But it jammed consistently with "stubbier" defensive cartridges.

Fortunately, technology has now caught up to both expanding ammunition and the more delicate design of the automatic pistol. Some very exotic and well-thought-out hollow-point defense ammo is available, and it leaves the magazine, goes up the ramp, and enters the chambers with sufficient reliability. (Nothing works 100 percent of the time.) At least in well-made pistols, the bullet then leaves the barrel, the brass flies out the ejection port, and you start the process all over again.

The advantages of the automatics are that they almost always hold more ammunition than a revolver, they are faster and easier to reload under stress, and, being flat-sided, they are somewhat easier and more comfortable to conceal. On the downside, however, this higher capacity causes some people to mistake their 10 to 15 rounds as an unlimited supply of ammunition and embrace the "spray and pray" philosophy—wasting all, hitting nothing. The other disadvantage, as already stated, is the more complex design of the automatic.

Let's look at the three basic types of autos, and then we'll touch on a couple that are neither "fish nor foul." The single-action auto (SA), if carried or stored with the hammer down, must be manually cocked before firing. Most professionals who choose the SA carry the weapon in the "cocked and locked" (hammer back, manual safety on) mode which requires only a simple downward movement of the thumb to unblock the firing pin. The single-action automatic is considered to be the fastest accurate automatic design on the market, and is used by the FBI, SWAT, Hostage Rescue Teams, U.S. Navy SEAL Team Six, and other specialty and counterterrorist units around the world.

Double-action (DA) automatics usually have a safety, which also sometimes acts as a decocking device—a really silly-ass contraption in my opinion. They may be carried quite safely with this safety disengaged, as they require a long, deliberate trigger pull on the first shot just like a DA revolver. Unless you choose to utilize the safety, the DAs are easier to bring into play than the SAs. They are, however, harder to bring into play with pinpoint accuracy because the long pull is usually hard and gritty and does not even approach the smoothness found in good DA revolvers. This can make the first round fired inaccurate. Subsequent shots revert to SA mode with a trigger pull now many pounds lighter than the first. Unless you have a great deal of conditioning to such sudden and drastic change, this can result in your firing the second shot sooner than desired under stress, quite possibly making it, too, a "throwaway."

The new kid on the block in automatics is the double-action-only (DAO) design. If you ask me, it was created more with litigation and liability in mind than pragmatic self-defense. In some cases people who have shot attackers in self-defense have faced manslaughter charges, with the prosecution's assumption being that the gun went off accidently. This is easier for prosecuting attorneys to argue if the weapon involved has a short, light trigger pull than a harder one. The DAOs feature the same deliberate, long, consistent trigger pull found on the DA's first shot every time the trigger is pulled. This makes each trigger pull uniform but, in turn, makes each stroke the hard kind that jerks through varying stages of drag and again spoils accuracy on every shot rather than just the first.

If you got the idea that I favor SA autos, you're right. I grew up with them, I've carried them for 25 years, and I'm used to both their advantages and disadvantages. But unlike many of my contemporaries, I do not particularly care for the 1911 Government Model .45. I find it difficult to point well (more about that later), although the Browning Hi-Power, a very similar design, seems to put the bullets exactly where I want them to go. When I'm carrying an auto, the Browning is indeed my first choice. The one I spoke of earlier (yes, the one that was such a picky ammo eater) has now had thousands and thousands of rounds run through it and has loosened up to the point that it will now reliably take any type of 9mm Parabellum known to man. (I'm not sure I couldn't make it work with .380s.) It's been retired, however, in favor of the same model now available in .40 S&W.

There are some exceptions to my prejudices against DAs and DAOs, however. Although it would not be my personal favorite, I could live with one of the Sig/Sauers. They are very well made and reliable (they should be, considering how much they cost), and of all the DA and DAO pistols, I find these to have the best trigger—even to the point of approaching the smoothness of a revolver. The DA-SA switch after the first shot is something to which anyone with the desire, and a willingness to practice, can become accustomed.

The Glock pistols, sometimes erroneously referred to as DAs, actually operate with what Glock calls a "safe action." There is no manual safety to be found on these guns; they don't need them. The trigger pull has a little different feel, but unless you get one of those appalling models they manufacture for the New York City Police Department, you can easily adjust to it. The Glock also points far better than most automatics, having a less-perpendicular barrel-to-grip angle than the majority of today's autos, which are patterned after the Government models. In short, Glocks have so many excellent features that I took it upon my gray-bearded-grandpa-getting-set-in-his-ways self to get used to them. I now own several.

Perhaps the most unusual design on the market today, and maybe the most underrated, is the Heckler & Koch P7 "squeeze cocker." This weapon, available in .380 auto, 9mmP, and .40 S&W, features a cocking device on the front strap of the grip that looks vaguely similar to the grip safety found on the back of the Government models. Simply grasping the weapon cocks it, and it may then be fired in SA mode. As soon as the grip is lightened, the gun is uncocked. P7s are simple, safe, and reliable. They are also quite expensive. I'm still kicking myself for selling mine—it once saved my life and the lives of my wife and son. No, not in self-defense; I sold it while in graduate school, and it put a little much-needed rice and beans on the table. Like the old saying goes, "You can't have your gun and eat it too."

Now that I've spouted off with my personal views about SA, DA, and DAO automatics, let me close with something that may make those of you who own and rely on weapons of this type feel a little better: since most defensive shootings take place at extremely close range, the inaccuracy caused by DA and DAO pistols is usually not enough to make it an issue. And for those of you who enjoyed disagreeing and were telling yourselves that it made no difference all along, don't worry. Some of you will have the opportunity to get mad all over again as soon as I start in on sighted versus aimed fire.

As I've already said, for most people, I believe the revolver is probably a better choice than an automatic for self-defense. The people I would say don't fall into this group are those who have an adequate amount of experience with automatics, and have also proven that they don't fall to pieces under stress. I would include myself in this group, as I have been involved in shootings with automatics and have never failed to remove a safety or hit my mark or fumbled the weapon in any way. Perhaps even more important, there have been many, many arrest situations in which I did not have to shoot but was forced to hold a light-triggered SA auto on someone (and don't let them fool you—cops in situations like this do not always keep their finger off the trigger or leave the safety engaged) without accidentally discharging the weapon. I think it is fairly safe to say that I have proven beyond a reasonable doubt, at least to myself, that I can keep a clear mind and stay in control during life-threatening encounters. Still, as a day-to-day carry gun, I choose a revolver. Why? I'm so glad you asked.

First and foremost, the revolver is simplicity itself. It is fast into action—you pull it out, aim it at what you want to hit, pull the trigger, and hit your target. It points better than the vast majority of automatics on the market, and there are no safeties to mess with. Yet it is safer than an SA automatic carried with the manual safety engaged. Even though automatics are far more reliable than they used to be, a revolver is still less likely to malfunction. (Of course, if the long shot comes through and it does malfunction, you may be in a world of hurt since it will be harder to clear than most auto jams.) The downside to wheel guns is their limited ammunition capacity. The vast majority are five- or six-shooters, although Taurus and Smith & Wesson are now making revolvers with seven and even eight holes in the cylinder (.22 revolvers sometimes hold even more). But for myself, at least, I feel this problem is more than offset by the fact that most self-defense shootings involve far fewer than six rounds. And it is self-defense we are talking about here, not Delta Force missions or SWAT team work. If I were still a full-time working police officer, you may believe that my 14-shot Glock 21 .45 ACP would be on my hip when I was in uniform and concealed somewhere on my body when I was in plain clothes. If I were still working undercover . . . well, that's another story.

There is no area of police work that relates as directly to civilian self-defense as undercover work. That's because the undercover officer is masquerading as a civilian, and his primary objective is to do his business and not get killed while he does it—just like yours. He is not concerned with making arrests; the arrests come later, after the warrants are issued, or are handled by his backup team if the suspects are to be taken into custody while he's still "under." The undercover officer carries weapons for the same reason civilians do—for self-defense. The fact that his daily environment is probably a lot more hostile than yours just means he stands a better chance of having to use that weapon. He also stands a much greater chance of getting into unarmed combat, and it always seems to happen fast, with little or no warning, just like civilian self-defense. Want a good, realistic, and legal way to test out your warrior mind-set and combat skills? Go become an undercover officer. Without the experiences I had during those years of my life, much of this book could not have been written. What? You say that doesn't interest you? Okay, then just read on.

My policy when working undercover was the same as my personal defense policy now. I carried a small- to medium-frame revolver, in those days a .38+P or a .44 Special, as my primary weapon. My only worry was that I was often outnumbered far more than five or six to one, and five or six shots was all I had. Now, forget the fact that if open gunplay had ensued under such circumstances, I would probably have been dead long before I could even pull the trigger five times. (Undercover officers who start thinking about such things wind up in a state hospital for a 90-day observation period.) No, just like you should do as a civilian concerned with self-defense, I adopted the warrior mind-set; I intended to survive. So I needed a plan as to what to do after my wheel gun ran dry.

My answer was the 14-round Browning as a backup. This was, and still is, a total reversal of the common wisdom, which states that the "big gun" should be the primary weapon, with a smaller gun in the backup role. My procedure (which was actually nothing more than a mind-set itself; who is to say which gun you will draw first in any given situation?) was frowned upon, and sometimes laughed at, by a few of my superiors (the ones I did, and still do, consider to actually be my "inferiors"). Their view, as always, was, "It's never been done that way before." But by then I had grown out of the "*Hai, Sensei!*" stage of police work, too, and their narrow-minded perspectives had little effect on me.

What I am saying is that this method of carry, and this mind-set, worked for me, with my specific needs. If it also works for you, fine—no charge except the price of the book. But if it doesn't apply to your specific condition or situation, like every other recommendation I make in this book, you should discard it. Think for yourself and work out your own system that does work for you.

Today, I most often leave the house with a five-shot Smith & Wesson Model 642 .357 magnum. It's small, wears Barami Hip-

Grips, making it simple to carry, and packs a darn good punch. When I'm dressed to hide it, and feeling "feistier," I might go with my six-holed Taurus .44 magnum with its three-inch barrel, or my "eight-shooter"—a Taurus of the same size in .357 magnum. Depends on my mood. I've carried most of the S&W revolvers at one time or another over the years and still don't think you can find any better wheel guns. But in the last few years Taurus has equaled them. Rossi firearms were getting pretty close, and now that they've teamed up with Taurus they're destined to become top of the line as well. Ruger is right up there too, but I've never liked the way Rugers felt in my hand for some reason. I still think the best revolver ever made is the Colt Python, and the Colt Detective Special is also a classic. But I wouldn't give you a nickel for all the other Colts on the market today. I'd have said that a lot more diplomatically if Colt weren't currently in bed with the gun control advocates. (What *are* you guys thinking, anyway?) The Browning .40 S&W auto goes in my JAGWEAR Concealment Systems briefcase, which features a panel with holster, magazine carriers, and other pockets that I use for a lightweight ASP collapsible baton and ASP laser flashlight suitable for striking an attacker, as well as blinding him temporarily by shining it in his eyes.

I tell you all this—and will do so with other weapons in the next few chapters—because this is the system that works for me. That does not mean it is automatically perfect for you. In fact, since you are not me, and you do not have my exact same life-style, it's highly unlikely that it would be. This is just to get you started thinking. Find your own systems for defense. Then be ready to modify them constantly because your life is in a constant state of flux, just like mine. By the time you read this, my revolvers and Browning may be in the closet, and I may be going with a whole new program.

SOME DANGEROUS MISCONCEPTIONS

There are a few things I'd like to address briefly before we move on to "how to shoot." First are some common, and very dangerous, misconceptions. Never believe that a gun in your hand will frighten an attacker into submission. If it does, great. Order him to the ground, hold him at gunpoint, and call the cops. But many people have died who purchased guns thinking, "I'll just scare him with it." The same applies to "I'll just shoot him in the leg." To be blunt, you're not that good. Shoot for center mass—*always*. If your attacker is wearing a protective vest, and your rounds appear only to stun him, switch to the head or pelvic area. If you are in fear of death or great bodily harm, you have a moral and legal right to take his life if necessary. If you are not, you have no right to shoot at all.

Never believe that any single round, regardless of caliber, will stop an attacker in his tracks. Aggressive attackers have been known to keep coming after taking truly unbelievable numbers of bullets— sometimes to vital organs. Shoot until the threat is over.

If you find yourself on the other end of the barrel, do not be one of those people who ignorantly say of small-caliber .22s and .25s, "If you shoot me with that, you'll just make me mad." While the .22 is hardly the defensive weapon of choice, more people die from .22-caliber wounds each year than from any other round. Likewise, keep in mind that a small-caliber gun in your hand is far better than *no gun* in your hand.

CONCEALED CARRY

If you are planning to carry a firearm with you and your state offers a concealed-carry permit, please get one. I, myself, am in favor of the system Vermont has, in which any legitimate citizen has the right to carry concealed without a permit. I also do not like the silly restrictions most states place on where and when the permit holder may carry. People who pass the prerequisite background investigations for such permits do not automatically turn into shooting maniacs when they enter a courthouse, school, or business with one of those stupid little stickers that feature a gun with a red circle around it and a slash through the middle. Much of the time, the places that are "off limits" are the very places you are most likely to need to protect yourself. Post offices? Schools? The people who carry guns into such places with evil intent do not bother with laws and do not qualify for permits, and if the good guys are following the law and are unarmed . . . well, we see what happens almost every day, don't we? Take the incident at Columbine High School in Littleton, Colorado, in April 1999. The little ghouls who killed 15 and wounded 19 more violated 19 existing gun laws. As this so clearly illustrates, people who choose to violate the law are not deterred by laws. That's why we call them outlaws.

But my opinion and a couple of bucks will get you a cup of coffee most places. I would never tell anyone to violate the law, but in this case I would never tell anyone *not* to violate a concealed-carry law if his life depended upon it. Personally, I never arrested anyone for carrying a weapon illegally unless they were also breaking some other, more serious law. But not all police officers think like I do. So, drink your coffee, make your decision, and take your chances if you find yourself needing to tote a gun but, for one reason or another, are forced to do so illegally.

How you carry your gun is a matter of personal life-style, body build, and several other factors—far too many to go into here. But there are more holsters and other means of carrying a gun on the market today than ever before. Evaluate your personal situation, then take your time and pick out what's best for you. Or do like I do and just buy every new gimmick that comes along. You can store the foolish choices in one of those big cardboard boxes in the attic until it's time for the garage sale. Since my primary reason for carrying a gun today is personal defense rather than police work, I find myself leaning more and more toward "simple and comfortable." Pocket holsters are high on my list these days, particularly during hot weather when a T-shirt or tank top may be all I'm wearing above the waist. And the Barami Hip-Grip, a modest little device that allows a small revolver to be carried without a holster at all, should not be overlooked. The bottom line is, after the novelty of carrying a gun wears off, it's more burden than amusement most days. Keeping things simple means you're more likely to have a weapon with you when you need it.

MODERN TECHNIQUE VS. POINT SHOOTING

I promised to give some of you a chance to get mad again,

remember? Well, here it comes. For the last several decades, police, military, and civilians have fallen victim to a method of shooting that is a very good way to punch holes in paper targets and make steel plates go "ding" but is not only impractical but dangerous for self-defense purposes. Yes, I'm afraid I'm talking about the popular "modern technique of the pistol."

I hold no misconceptions that what I am about to say will sink into the heads of the died-in-the-wool "front sight" shooters. In fact, you've already tuned me out, haven't you? But if you are not a die-hard "true believer" of this system or one of those shooting instructors with all your money (and your very name) invested in this approach who doesn't dare admit your mistake now (or even if you fall into one of these categories but have an open mind, are not threatened by opposing ideas, and would rather survive a gunfight than die stubbornly defending your theory, which has proven time and time again, in countless law enforcement shootings, to be false), read on.

For those of you who are new shooters, or for the sake of anyone not already familiar with the modern "always-use-your-sights" method, let's do a little experiment. Stand up, get a handgun, check to be sure it's unloaded, check it again, and face a safe direction. Shuffle your feet into what is called a Weaver stance (it's sort of a way of standing sideways at about a 45-degree angle to the direction you are facing, left foot forward if you are right-handed). Now grip the gun in both hands—not too light, but not too hard, either. Bring it up to your eyes. Find the sights. Breathe in, then let half of your breath out. Push toward your target with your strong hand (the one with which you will operate the trigger) and pull back against that pressure with your weak hand to create an isometric tension to assist in recoil control. Pick out a target on the wall in front of you but do not look directly at it. Let the target blurr in the background; focus your eyes on that front sight! Now, *s-q-u-e-e-z-e* that trigger; don't pull it.

Finished? How did you do? Pretty well? Good. It's really not too hard to put all those things together there in your living room or bedroom, is it?

Now, get someone to stand across the room with a loaded gun

and start shooting at you and see if you can still do all those things while he tries to kill you.

The "modern technique" has spread like wildfire over the last several decades for two reasons. First, because it works so well in the shooting sports. It is the system used by competitive shooting champions the world over, and without adopting it you will never win a trophy. But we are not talking about shooting paper, steel, or bowling pins here; we are talking about high-stress, life-and-death self-defense encounters during which you are very likely to be getting shot at while you shoot. In the gun games, if you lose you go home depressed. In a gunfight, if you lose you don't go home at all. Yes, the "modern technique" is unbeatable on the practice range and in the shooting sports. But do you remember my stressing the difference between the dojo and the street in the last chapter? The same difference applies here; just change dojo to firing range. Gun games relate to gunfights only in that guns are used in both. The procedures used to win a trophy are only slightly more applicable to self-defense than those used in golf or tennis.

The second reason the "modern technique" has caught on is that it was in the right place at the right time. Original handgun training—military, police, and civilian alike—involved primarily bullseye shooting. Point shooting enjoyed a period of popularity among law enforcement trainers during the post-World War II era, as evidenced in old FBI and other training films. But in those days, the average police officer went his entire career without drawing his weapon except on the range, and those range sessions were few and far between. Even when I entered law enforcement in the mid-1970s, state law required an officer to qualify *once* with a revolver, and he was never required to do so again. I recall one man who had probably been a rookie deputy when Wyatt Earp was sheriff and had not fired a gun in more than 20 years. When I asked to see what he carried one day, he handed me a revolver that contained cartridges so corroded that the cylinder could not be opened. Even more amazing, when I pointed this out to him, he shrugged and placed it back in his holster. This, of course, was not true everywhere, but it was far more widespread in those days than most people realize.

Then the new wave of violence that is still growing in our society commenced. More and more shootings began to take place, and more and more officers began missing what they were shooting at and getting shot themselves. Police administrators dropped the culpability at the foot of the curriculum at the time instead of placing the blame where it belonged—on the fact that far too many officers had never learned *any* system of shooting. Consider now the fact that certain "combat" shooting sports like International Practical Shooting Competition (IPSC) and Practical Pistol Competition (PPC) were gaining popularity, and the logic they followed becomes clear: the sportsmen were hitting their targets far more often than the cops were; therefore, they must be doing it the right way.

The real problem that caused trainers to confuse sport with reality (just as martial artists have confused dojo and street) was the simple fact that it had been too long since we'd had a war in which the handgun played a vital part. While Vietnam was still in the near past, the M16 and shotgun had been used far more frequently than the pistol. But ask the few Vietnam vets who did employ the handgun regularly if they ever had both hands free to take a two-handed grip. Ask the "tunnel rats" who crawled through mile after mile of underground darkness if they could even see their front sights, let alone try to focus on them. Ask the men from World War II's trenches if they shifted into the Weaver stance, took a deep breath, then let half of it out before shooting.

Everything about the "modern technique" violates the human being's natural instincts in the face of danger. When the body is threatened with immediate physical harm, it intuitively tries to make itself a smaller target and protect its vital areas by crouching—not standing upright and turning sideways. The eyes focus directly on the threat—not the front sights of a firearm. As we discussed in Chapter 2, small muscle skills—like those required to gently squeeze rather than pull a trigger—diminish. Heart rate increases, hard and fast, and this in itself means that taking a deep breath and letting out half of it while doing all the other things promoted by this system is, while not impossible, very improbable.

So is it possible to develop this "modern technique" well enough to make it a viable method for self-defense? To paraphrase

Mr. Toguchi's words, of course it is possible. Elite military and police units around the world do it all the time. All you have to do is completely retrain your body so that the unnatural becomes natural. This *can* be done. Of course it will require firing several hundred rounds a day over the next few years. But don't worry; after that you can slack off to two to three days a week to keep up your newly acquired skill. Anything less and you'll revert back to doing what's natural for a human being rather than behaving like a programmed robot.

What's that? You have a job you've got to go to? A family you want to spend time with? Want to read a book or watch a movie once in a while? Then perhaps you should read this next section about point shooting.

First, let me give you a definition of point shooting (both what it is and what it is not) and a brief history of its proven success. Then we'll look at the basics, which are really very simple.

Point shooting, while it is not sighted fire, is most definitely aimed fire. It is most definitely not the same as hip shooting, as many of the current "modern technique" instructors, who know better, would lead you to believe in order to further their own interests. Hip shooting is a very small part of the system, but it is used only at extremely close range—about arm's distance. The "modern technique" folks have their own version of unsighted fire for such close quarters, called the "speed rock." It doesn't work any better or worse than hip shooting; it's just more complicated, as things always are with the "modern" folks.

Point shooting is based on the fact that you learned to point your finger as a child and have perfected that ability ever since. It recognizes that while the old adage "it doesn't matter how fast you are if you don't hit what you're shooting at" is true, it is no more true than "it won't matter how accurate you are if you're too slow." While "reasonable" accuracy in combat shooting is essential, "pinpoint" shot placement is not and requires too much wasted time. Point shooting takes into consideration the fact that, as Siddle and others have scientifically proven, your fine motor skills will have deserted you, requiring you to rely on simple techniques that involve gross motor movement if you are to survive. It also incorporates the body's other natural reactions to danger—such as the desire to crouch—rather than fighting them or attempting to change them.

In short, point shooting goes with the flow. The "modern technique" bucks the waves.

There is evidence that would lead us to believe that point shooting was indeed the method of combat pistolcraft practiced by the successful Old West gunfighters. During World War II, a young lieutenant by the name of Rex Applegate was assigned by Office of Strategic Services (OSS, the forerunner of today's CIA) Director William "Wild Bill" Donovan to "learn everything there is to know about close-quarters combat." During the course of his studies, Lieutenant Applegate discovered an old letter written by Wild Bill Hickock. In this letter, Hickock described the technique he employed in gunfights:

"I raised my hand to eye-level, like pointing a finger, and fired."

There is no better short definition of point shooting to be found anywhere.

Together with British officers Anthony Sykes and W.E. Fairbairn, Applegate began to perfect point shooting. Thousands of American OSS operatives, U.S. Army intelligence officers, and British Commandos and Home Guard personnel were trained in point shooting and sent out on missions. They reported back to their trainers what had worked and what had not. Time and time again, the point shooting system proved effective. It has continued to do so over the more than 50 years since World War II ended.

My uncle, Gene Gott, originally taught me this system of shooting when I was around 5 years old. A Korean War vet and fan of Colonel (by that time) Applegate's book *Kill or Get Killed*, my Uncle Gene had watched me draw and hip-shoot my toy six-shooters as I had seen Roy Rogers, Gene Autry, Sunset Carson, and all my other heroes do in the movies and on television. One day he said, "That's pretty good. But would you like to learn the real way to shoot?" We replaced the six-shooter with a dart gun, found some toy soldiers, and lined them up on the low mantle above the fireplace. He then taught me the basics of point shooting, and I'd like to pass on what he taught me to you now:

1) Face your target squarely and look straight at it.
2) Keep both eyes open.
3) Raise the gun in front of you with a straight arm, like you would if you were pointing your finger. Pull the trigger as soon as it reaches eye level.
4) Hold the dart gun tight, because real guns have a "kick" to them.

That, folks, is how simple it is. Even a child can learn the basics with a dart gun.

I don't recall my uncle talking about crouching that day. He may very well have, but if he did, it didn't sink into my 5-year-old mind. Then again, after his death, I found a copy of Bill Jordan's *No Second Place Winner* in his library. Although this famous quick-draw point-shooting U.S. Border Patrolman's book wasn't published until several years after my first point-shooting lesson, it's possible that Uncle Gene, like Jordan, had decided on his own that if you could train yourself not to crouch you would save a few hundredths of a second. Now, I would never argue with anyone of Bill Jordan's abilities. But it should be pointed out that this is the only difference between his method and Colonel Applegate's, and that Jordan was an exhibition shooter who did indeed practice enough to overcome the natural desire to crouch. Most of us, I believe, should be very wary about changing things in the point-shooting system; as soon as you start fighting any of your natural instincts in the face of danger rather than flowing with them, you're on your way to starting your own impractical "modern" method.

As this book goes to press, several law enforcement agencies, primarily due to the efforts of the late Colonel Applegate, are beginning to return to their senses. They are finally recognizing that the percentage of hits compared to shots fired by their officers (annually 14–16 percent) is abysmal. Recently the BATF and the California State Patrol have realized that we have tried to fix something that was not broken, and both agencies have returned to point shooting for their officers. We can only hope that the rest of the law enforcement agencies will follow this lead.

If you want to spend countless time and money learning the

"modern technique," who am I to tell you not to do so? In the end, you will shoot a little more accurately than a point shooter who practices for 30 minutes once or twice a year. It won't be enough to make any difference in self-defense, and it won't be enough so that you'll ever be completely certain you'll do it all right when the chips are down. But it might come in handy on your next top-secret mission to Iraq in which Saddam Hussein is holding your wife hostage in front of you at 30 paces and you have only the top left quarter of his face as a target. Be realistic. If you are a civilian interested in practical self-defense or a police officer or soldier without unlimited time and ammunition, go the point-shooting route. When the feces hit the oscillator, you'll be glad you did. I always was.

THE FAST DRAW

One of the most important—yet overlooked and sometimes even scorned—aspects of firearms self-defense is the fast draw. To some it conjures up images of cowboys and gun nuts, and even gun writers these days have come up with a "politically correct" term for it. They call it "the presentation." Ugh! You "present" your gun if you like; I believe I'll just continue to draw mine, thank you.

Now, everyone has heard stories about people shooting themselves in the foot practicing the fast draw. This does happen, but it can be avoided with a little common sense. In any case, the citizen, cop, or soldier who ignores the fast draw is cutting down his chances of survival immeasurably. If you ever really do need a weapon, you are really likely to need it really fast. Learning to pull your gun from the holster, pants, or purse with speed is essential, particularly at the close range of the average self-defense situation.

For the civilian, the fast draw is even more important than for the cop or soldier. Cops have a saying that the fastest draw is already having the gun in your hand. This is true, but they can get away with it in many situations in which a civilian would be arrested for "brandishing a firearm." And even a cop doesn't always get enough forewarning to draw his gun ahead of time.

My advice is to begin very slowly, practicing a smooth draw with

Pellet and BB pistols offer a cheap, safe, and convenient way to practice defensive shooting in your own backyard. The gun in the author's hand is a Gamo R77. The holstered revolver is the Crossman 357. Both are excellent training tools.

an *unloaded* weapon and letting speed take care of itself. Speed is acquired by lessening wasted effort, and indeed the fastest gunmen actually look like they're putting no effort into the act at all. Trying to force speed only creates clumsiness, and numerous repetitions will be necessary before you are drawing fast and uniformly and bringing the gun up to eye level. So remember that mysterious Oriental Zen secret Bruce Lee used: work at it.

When you feel you have made adequate progress with an empty weapon, go buy a pellet pistol that resembles your handgun of choice as closely as possible. With it you can begin actually drawing and firing without the risk of having to limp into the emergency room and tell the doctor how stupid you are. Pellets are also a very economical way to practice both speed and accuracy, as well as all other aspects of gunplay except recoil control.

I myself train regularly in my backyard with two .177-caliber pellet revolvers: a 4″ Crossman "357" and a 2 1/2″ Gamo R77.

Paper plates serve as excellent makeshift targets for backyard shooting practice with pellet and BB pistols.

Both are excellent training devices, but each has advantages and disadvantages. The full-size Crossman holds 10 rounds and can be quickly reloaded with its particular version of "speed loaders." But it has a longer barrel than the guns I usually carry for simple self-defense. The Gamo is smaller and patterned very much like a Smith & Wesson Model 19/66. It actually feels much closer to my usual defense weapons, but while it holds eight rounds, it's considerably slower to reload. For targets, I tack paper plates to trees at varying heights to represent chests and heads and scatter them around to create multiple attackers. (Then I lie to my wife about what happened to all the paper plates come picnic time.)

When I go to the firing range, the majority of my practice is done from the ready (gun in hand, angled down and ready to raise) position. I limit myself to no more than 20 loaded "quick draw and fire" repetitions at any one session—even when I feel like doing more. Sometimes, if I am distracted or feel my mind wandering, I stop far short of the 20 reps. Actually drawing and firing a loaded high-caliber firearm at top speed is a serious undertaking and should never be practiced to the point where carelessness might set in. As in other defensive training, you must acquire most of your skill in pieces: drawing an unloaded gun, drawing and firing your pellet trainer, firing your actual carry weapon from the ready position, and so on. What you learn from each specific aspect will then carry over to help create the entire defensive shooting process, which consists of mind-set and muscle memory.

As we move on, keep in mind that shooting is no different than any other means of self-defense. We must follow as closely as possible what our bodies and spirits tell us to do, changing or modifying only those details that are absolutely necessary to make our techniques effective for specific situations. If your heart tells you a certain program, or a certain technique within that program, will not be effective, chances are good that it won't be—at least for you. Just as the martial arts of ancient times were designed for specific people, places, and weapons and are not always practical for individuals training for self-defense today, so some of the shooting techniques you're exposed to in today's world will not be appropriate for you and your specific needs. So listen to your heart; it's there to keep you alive in more ways than just pumping blood through your system.

Let us permit nature to have her way: she understands her business better than we do.

—Michel de Montaigne
Essays, III, 1588

6

Knives

Give Yourself an Edge

The sword is the weapon of the brave.
—Napoleon I to Gaspard Gourgaud
at St. Helena, c. 1816

This is as good a place as any to explain the differences between edged, impact, and extension weapons. Edged weapons (as you may already have guessed, you sly devil, you) have a sharp edge that cuts. They are capable of creating lacerations and, if they also include a point, punctures. Yes—like a knife. Impact weapons are blunt objects that crush rather than cut. They break bones, knock out teeth, and leave bruises, although if the skin is actually broken at the point of impact, these wounds become what we call abrasions. When you think of impact weapons, think ballpeen hammer or baseball bat. Extension weapons "reach out and touch someone" at a distance, and again you can think of the old Louisville slugger you wish you could use like Mark McGuire. Usually, 16 inches is considered the minimum length for extension weapons.

As we saw with the baseball bat, many weapons fall into more than one category. Make the bat out of steel and put an edge on it and you then have a weapon that possesses the characteristics of all three groups. (Of course most of us call those things swords instead of "sharp bats.") A hatchet is an edged-impact weapon. But lengthen the handle and turn it into an axe, and it now adds the new dimension and versatility of extension.

Knives are, of course, edged and, more often than not, pointed. If they are long enough, like true bowies, full-size Japanese tantos, and a few other designs, they are also extension weapons. Most knives can be used to create blunt trauma, as well. The flat sides of the blade, the back edge of a single-edged knife, the guard that separates the handle from the blade, and the pommel (butt end) are all capable of being used as impact weapons. On the surface, knives seem like the most rudimentary of weapons, but they are really very versatile little critters.

I have already stated that I believe the firearm to be the best weapon for self-defense in today's society. Now, let me "waffle" a bit (call me Slick Jerry if you like) and state that there are times when I'd rather have a knife for self-defense. Within their range, blades have some distinct advantages over guns. First, you are not going to overpenetrate your target and kill an innocent person unfortunate enough to be standing behind your attacker. Second, keep in mind that with firearms, the real weapon is the bullet, not the gun. As soon as it leaves the barrel, you are no longer in control of that weapon. Bullets have a nasty tendency to develop minds of their own, playing little tricks that never seemed possible to you in the split second you had to decide whether to pull the trigger or not. If you miss, it's even worse than overpenetration. Bullets can ricochet up, down, and all around, and ruin the day (or life) of anyone ill-fatedly standing in their path. A missed knife slash or thrust is not likely to produce consequences nearly as dire since the weapon remains in your hand and under your control. In crowded environments, or in houses or apartments with thin walls through which even low-velocity bullets may pass, this can be a real advantage.

Now, let me take another step toward the deep end and really get some of you riled. At close range, and by that I mean arm's length and one step, even in the middle of a wheat field with no innocent bystanders or anyone else around, I would rather have the right big knife than any handgun ever invented.

We've all heard that tired old joke about taking a knife to a gun-fight. But there are a lot of assumptions made in that story, and few of them ring true on the street. First, the great majority of self-defense situations begin at very close range. Just as there are few drive-by kickings, few attackers halt in the middle of the sidewalk 50 feet from their victim and announce their intentions. Firearms buffs talk a lot about "stopping power," which is basically how likely a first shot is to shut down the attacker's nervous system or otherwise force him to cease and desist. If this interests you, I highly recommend Evan Marshall and Ed Sanow's books *Handgun Stopping Power* and *Street Stoppers*. But the bottom line is, even if you do your part and place your bullet precisely, no handgun round is 100-percent effective; some people just haven't watched enough TV to know they're sup-posed to lie down and die as soon as they're shot. (This precondi-tioned psychological reaction to being shot is far more prevalent than many people understand.) Stopping power comes from sudden impact trauma and wound channel size, and the wound channel that can be created by a long thick blade with a "thrust and pump" action is truly astonishing. I had always known this in theory, but it was driven home to me in fact, up close and personal, a few months ago.

Ever heard of these wild boar knife hunts? "Whoa!" you say, "not me! Those things have sharp teeth and tusks and they're mean!" Well, I thought the same thing. That's why I went on one last sum-mer looking for a little adventure to break the day-to-day monotony of sitting in front of this computer. I jokingly told my wife that it was a middle-aged male thing, and that I either had to do this or find a younger woman on the side. She told me to go ahead; there was a chance I'd survive the boar, but she'd make sure I got hurt if I chose the younger woman. Anyway, it did not turn out to be much of an adventure. Wild boars are not all that wild after they've been chased by trained pit bulls until they're about to die of a heart attack. And stabbing an animal, regardless of how ferocious it may be, while three or four of the dogs hold it in place for you, does not qualify as a death-defying act in my book. In truth, if I hadn't already paid my money and figured I might as well get the meat, I'd have said forget it and let the poor thing go. (If you'd prefer a more romantic version of this escapade, I can put you in touch with a couple of guys who were along that day. They're still swaggering and bragging about their "near death" experience and love nothing better than letting the story grow a little with each telling.)

As I see it, only one good thing came from the whole pathetic ordeal: I thrust the 12-inch spear-point blade of a Jim Keating/Bob Dozier Crossada into the heart of a 350-pound wild animal, and it bled out and died within what I'd estimate to be two to three seconds. The guides told me they had never seen any bullet put one down that fast, and I don't believe anything short of a 12-gauge slug could. Now, consider the fact that the hog's chest was at least twice as big around as most men's, and the fact that wild animals rarely watch much television (they're too busy reading), so they aren't mentally preconditioned to fall down and die. Now you get the picture of what even a 5- to 7-inch blade can do to a human "animal." Overall, I really think we give bullets too much credit for stopping power and blades too little.

For many people in today's society, a knife may be the best answer as a defensive weapon. Although I know of no state that issues a permit to carry knives that violate its statutes (that doesn't mean one doesn't exist; it very well may), if you stay within the laws of the jurisdiction, no permit is necessary. Employers who have policies against their employees being armed at work (and the way some of them treat their employees, they have every reason to be worried) are usually concerned with firearms; such restrictions are rarely extended to small and/or folding knives or any knives that are obviously used on the job. In other words, both legally and socially, you can often carry a knife—at least the right kind of knife—at times and in places where a firearm would be forbidden.

LEGAL AND SOCIAL CONSIDERATIONS

On the other hand, let's talk about what you're likely to face after using a knife to legally defend yourself. The knife's image is not good in the eye of the general public. Some people who would pat you on the shoulder and say "Good job" if you shot someone in self-defense will look at you as if you are a deranged serial killer after you've cut the same person under the same set of circumstances. Don't ask me why; it makes absolutely no sense at all in my mind. But I see this attitude every day and recognize its presence. Many cops, prosecutors, and judges fall into this category. And you may be sure that a jury will include at least a few men or women who do not understand that life is life and death is death, and the tool you choose with which to preserve your life is not relevant to the legality or morality of your actions. In a sense, the burden of proof, which by law is on the prosecution, will be shifted to the defense. Right or wrong (and it's definitely wrong), you and your attorney are going to have to work doubly hard to prove that you had no other recourse.

Largely because we have been erroneously taught to think of the blade as the "bad guy's" weapon, the problem most people have with using a knife in self-defense is mental. Well, let's get something straight: a knife is a knife, just like a gun is a gun, and both are inanimate objects, just like teakettles. They do not possess the mentality or spirituality to be good or evil in and of themselves, and you would think this was something anyone over the age of about four would have figured out for themselves. But even people who should know better—even some people in the knife industry itself—promote this idea.

Recently, I shook my head in disbelief at an article in one of the "knife magazines." The writer, an ex-cop like myself, stated that he had faced knives many times during his law enforcement career. He also stated he had never wanted to take another human life unless absolutely necessary (and we'll pass right by, without comment, the fact that this goes without saying among most civilized people). In addition, he made it clear he did not consider the loss of his own life as criteria to qualify the taking of another life as absolutely necessary. Now that's either a lie, or he suffers from unbelievably low self-esteem. What police academy did *he* go to? They taught me—and I had no trouble accepting—that if there had to be somebody who wasn't going home after the shift, it should be the bad guy. Be that as it may, this police paragon of virtue didn't seem to mind using his nightstick to beat the living daylights out of suspects armed with knives. But ever use a knife for defense himself? Heavens, no! Knives are "remarkable beautiful friends!" They're works of art that shouldn't be lowered to the job of protecting mere human life.

Hey, guy? Grow up. Knives are nothing more than wood or rubber or plastic handles attached to a piece of sharp steel. Yes, you can grow fond of the better ones, and yes, some knives qualify as works of art, masterpieces of form or function, and sometimes both. But my life is a work of art too, and it's worth more to me than the whole ceiling of the Sistine Chapel.

PSYCHOLOGICAL CONSIDERATIONS

Beyond the mental blocks that often result from negative socialization regarding knives, using a knife does take a little different mind-set than a gun. I think the best way to put this into perspective is to first look at a few defense situations in their psychological extremes, then see where the knife falls into that picture. At the most impersonal level, a soldier sits at a control panel and pushes a button to launch a missile at his enemies, or a pilot flies over a site and drops a bomb on unseen faces. They not only don't see their victims die, they've never seen them at all, so in a sense they are not real casualties. Slightly below this on our scale is the sniper. He views his prey through a telescope at long range, then pulls the trigger, watches the man go down, and goes home. He sees the target fall and may even be able to ascertain that he is dead. But this still takes place at extreme distance, through a scope—sort of like watching it happen on television.

At the other end of the spectrum, we find face-to-face unarmed combat. I'm not talking about the playground fistfight here; I'm talking about a situation in which the other person is trying to kill you and the only way to keep that from happening is to kill him first. In a scenario such as this, your face may be two inches from his, and you may very well be looking him in the eye while you take his life with your bare hands. This is, indeed, up close and personal. Therefore, it is far more likely to cause anyone not mentally prepared in advance to hesitate, and it's also more likely to have emotional ramifications after the fact.

Shooting someone within typical handgun defense distance is more personal than dropping a bomb or even shooting someone with a sniper's rifle. But it's less personal than killing someone in unarmed combat. Even at contact range, all you do is pull a trigger. The bullet does the rest.

The mind-set it takes to cut, and particularly to stab, someone is very close to that which it takes to kill someone with your bare hands. But it may even seem more personal. Killing someone with your hands usually involves strangulation or blunt trauma; if the person bleeds it won't be much. Edged weapons bring about blood—sometimes lots of blood. Blood is messy and has always been a "gross out" for some people, but in today's era of blood-born pathogens like the HIV virus, only a complete fool doesn't understand that the danger involved goes beyond getting sick to your stomach. Keep in mind that a person who attacks you without just cause is also very likely to engage in other less-than-moral acts. He may well be an intravenous drug user. It is also pretty unlikely that he has strong feelings against promiscuous sex, wouldn't you assume? (In fact, he may even tell an occasional fib!) But also keep in mind that while AIDS continues to spread, the odds are still in favor of his not being infected. And I don't know about you, but if I have to make a choice, I'd rather die five or ten years from now than during his attack.

So do what you have to do, when you have to do it, and then do a lot of praying while you wait on the lab work. There are some fairly complex mental and emotional issues to work through here, so work through them *now*. If you wait until the time of the attack, you may well hesitate for that vital microsecond that means the difference between life and death.

About two years ago I had a very interesting conversation with a former Navy SEAL. Now, this is a guy for whom I have a lot of respect, and who understands combat well. So I think he was just having a bad day, or that his mind must have been on something else, because he said something he should have known better than to say.

"I'm not going to get into a knife fight with somebody and get AIDS," he said. "I'd just shoot them from a distance."

Now, this man is still pretty young. He entered the service after Vietnam, got out before Desert Storm, and somehow missed Panama and the other little war games in between. As far as I know he's never had to kill anybody with any weapon. But he is well trained enough that he should be aware that you rarely get to choose the rules of engagement in self-defense. Although he is one of the best fighters I know, if attacked he is not going to be any different from anyone else in that he probably won't have the opportunity to back away far enough to avoid the residual blood that comes from a close-quarters shooting. Believe me, you are going to get more blood on you if you shoot someone within knife range than if you cut their throat or stab them in the heart and then get out of the jet spray as fast as you can.

In addition to the fear of blood, there seems to be a resistance to thrusting the knife as opposed to cutting with it. Military close-quarters combat instructors are rampant with stories of trainees who quickly learned to slash with a bayonet but recoiled at the idea of thrusting—even into bloodless dummies. In every knife defense class I have ever taught, I have seen some of the same faces that remained deadpan when practicing slashes grow pale when training turned to the thrust. There may be some deep-seeded sexual aspects to this, but I also suspect part of it is that we know instinctively that thrusts are more deadly. Most slashes, if not to a vital area like an artery, can be treated. A thrust is much harder to survive.

PRINCIPLES OF KNIFE DEFENSE

Which brings us to one of the knife's best features—its versatility. Being both an impact and edged weapon, the knife can be used at different threat levels. Remember that obnoxious brother-in-law we talked about earlier who got drunk at the wedding reception? What if he happens to be six feet, five inches tall and weigh 250 pounds, and you're five-seven and 130? Lightly striking his rib cage with the blunt end of a closed folding knife may be helpful in getting his attention. Then jamming it against a nerve to assist the arm bar that escorts him out into the fresh air will help him sober up. He may

One advantage of the knife as a defensive weapon is that it gives gives you a wider range of options than a gun. A couple of quick slashes may be enough to change the mind of an aggressor who thought you looked like easy prey. With guns, there is no "bargain point."

then be more willing to hear your explanation of why there's a right way and a wrong way to kiss the bride, and the way he did it was definitely wrong. Even in more serious situations, the knife is often useful as an impact weapon. If you carry a folder, you may have time to draw but not open it before you are attacked. I had to hit a guy on top of the head with a closed Puma Trail Boss years ago, and that was enough to end the problem.

Once the knife is opened, a quick slash or two may be enough to change the mind of the aggressor who thought you were easy prey. In the Filipino systems of defense, they talk about the "bargain point." This is it. You may (notice I said *may*) be able to step back and ask your attacker if he's ready to call it quits or if he'd prefer being cut a few more times. This is not only the moral thing to do if you can, it shows restraint on your part later if you wind up in court. Can you imagine trying to do this with a gun?

In a serious encounter, and, as always, by that I mean one in

Regardless of what you've seen on TV and in the movies, flying side kicks and spinning back fists are not the way to handle multiple attack. Taking one of the assailants into the "bargain position," as shown here with a knife, is often the only sensible solution. When possible, taking the "leader" of the group hostage is always the best strategy. The trick is to keep from killing him and losing your advantage while negotiations take place.

which you stand to die or receive great bodily harm, you must, as Captain Fairbairn said, ". . . be more ruthless than your enemy." Many people, however, who have developed the warrior mind-set but are still uninitiated to the way of the knife make the mistake of going for the kill immediately. They attempt to thrust into the chest cavity or cut the throat (both vital areas that the human animal protects instinctively) while the attacker is still operating at 100-percent capacity. Hock Hochheim, head of the American Congress of Knife Fighters (and another former flatfoot who believes civilians have as much right to protect themselves as cops) often speaks of what he calls the "rule of the diminishing fighter." In other words, you have to wear your opponent down gradually before ending the confrontation. Now don't get me wrong—if an opportunity for a finishing strike presents itself early in the engagement, by all means take advantage of it. But this is an infrequent stroke of luck—the exception rather than the rule. Just as boxers rarely attempt a knockout with their first punch, it is usually not a good idea to do so with a knife. Any "knockout," and by that I again mean a final, finishing technique, takes a little longer to execute well. The boxer leads with short, fast jabs to set up the more powerful but harder-to-land cross or hook. In the same sense, you may have to create an opening for your grand finale with a few quick cuts or slashes with the knife. The Filipino arts put much emphasis on limb destruction, following the elementary but accurate principle that a man with a broken arm cannot swing very well, and a man with a broken leg has a very hard time kicking with it. Another of the Filipino doctrines is to "defang the snake." That means that if your opponent is armed, his weapon is your primary concern. Neutralize your attacker's means of hurting you first. Then, if it is still necessary, go after the attacker himself. The same applies when you employ a stick or any other hand-held weapon except a pistol—separate your attacker from the use of his weapon first. With a firearm, you go for the knockout right out of the gate. Only the Lone Ranger shoots the gun out of the bad guy's hand.

CHOICES IN DEFENSIVE KNIVES

Just as no gun is perfect for every self-defense situation, neither is any one knife. If you live in a jurisdiction where possessing a firearm is illegal or made so difficult that it becomes impractical, a large knife may become your choice for home defense. Big knives are also great for auto-carry defense, camping trips, and other appropriate outdoor activities. My personal favorite large knives are the bowie, smatchet, and Keating/Dozier Crossada.

Now "bowie" means different things to different people, so let me be a little more clear. I'm talking about a clip point blade of at least 9 1/2 inches, razor-sharp on both the primary and back edge. Very serviceable commercial bowies are available from Cold Steel, Gerber, Al Mar, Ontario, and a few other manufacturers. If you want the very best fighting bowie available, give custom knife maker Bill Bagwell a call and ask for one of his Hell's Belles. Much like a tailor would do, Bill will take your measurements, and the finished product will be a fighting knife beyond equal that is perfectly balanced and fitted specifically to you like a good suit. Other custom bowies of which I am very fond, which are a little less expensive, are the models put out by Randall Knives and by Ernest Mayer at Black Cloud Knives. There are other quality custom bowie makers, and I regret that limited space prevents me from listing them all.

The Applegate-Fairbairn Smatchet is a dynamic defense weapon that was issued to OSS operatives during World War II. It has a very wide, leaf-shaped 10-inch blade that cuts, chops, slices, and dices so well it should have its own infomercial. It also makes a very big and nasty wound when thrusting is employed. My personal Smatchet was manufactured by Al Mar Knives, but these are no longer being produced. (You might try gun and knife shows.) Boker Baumwerk-Solingen contracted with Colonel Applegate to produce this design, however, and by the time this book comes out they may well be on the market. In the meantime, an authorized custom model is available from William W. Harsey.

We now come to the Crossada designed by Master at Arms Jim Keating and made by Bob Dozier. It's sort of a cross between a bowie and an Arkansas Toothpick dagger, and I can personally vouch for its effectiveness. So can the wild boar's head on the wall just behind me. It glares at me every day, reminding me that I didn't fight fair, but also reminding me of the destruction of which that 12-inch double-edged spear-point blade is capable.

These are by no means the only good big knives. While there are several top-quality production companies making a few models, none of them offers as wide a variety of top-quality products as Cold Steel. Besides the Trailmaster Bowie, the Tai Pan (7 1/2-inch dagger), Black Bear classic (8 1/4-inch sub-hilt fighter), and R1 Military classic (a 7-inch replica of the classic Randall Model 1) are my personal favorites. And if tantos are your thing, Cold Steel has more variations than I have room here to talk about.

While knives with 7- to 12-inch blades are concealable in a variety of ways, it's somewhat difficult to do so, uncomfortable, and illegal almost everywhere. Even in jurisdictions in which open carry of fixed blades is permissible, knives of this size are rarely seen hanging from belts, and you may rest assured it will raise the eyebrows of citizens and law enforcement personnel alike. Drawing such attention to yourself is kind of stupid, don't you think? The people who don't scream and flee from you will write you off as a looney-toon, and anyone who decides to attack you will make certain he does so before you are able to access your weapon.

So most of us turn to small to medium folders or fixed blades for daily defense carry. My single most carried fixed blade is a Harsey-made custom Applegate-Fairbairn with a 6-inch dagger blade. If I am going to be in a situation where there's a better-than-usual chance of losing it (camping, hunting, whatever), I switch to the more economical, yet also excellent, Boker production knife of the same design. For me, the A-F is the best compromise between effective size and ease of concealed carry. Recently, during hot weather, which means fewer and lighter clothes, I have experimented with Boker's new A-F boot knife—same design but shrunken to a 4 3/4-inch blade. It is easier to carry, but I miss that extra inch and a quarter.

What Cold Steel is to fixed blades, Spyderco is to the folding knife; no one turns out as many different models suitable for self-defense. Spyderco's one-hand opening hole and pocket clip revolutionized the defensive knife industry and turned many a confirmed fixed blade carrier to the folder. I carried a Spyderco Police Model for many years, and even today it is a very rare occurrence when I leave the house without at least one "Spyder knife" clipped on me somewhere. I am also quite fond of Cold Steel's El Hombre, Extra-Large Voyager, and Vaquero Grande, and Gerber's Applegate-Fairbairn Combat and Applegate-Fairbairn Covert folders. Benchmade, SOG, Al Mar, Columbia River, and other production companies also make high-quality defense folders. Again, there are too many good production folder companies to mention them all. But this is a good place to reemphasize my theme about thinking for yourself and making your own decisions. The folder that is right for me may not be right for you, so shop the market and handle a few before you decide.

The Gerber E-Z Out is perhaps the best bargain on the market

The downside of folding knives is their strength and size. The upside is that you'll probably have it with you when you need it while your bowie will be at home. Some of the best are shown here. Left, top to bottom: Cold Steel Gunsite, Vaquero, and XL Voyager; Benchmade Balisong; Chris Reeves Sebenza. Right, top to bottom: Spyderco Civilian and Police, Columbia River Knife and Tool Apache, Gerber Applegate-Fairbairn Covert, Al Mar Backup. Bottom: Applegate-Fairbairn Combat Folder autographed by Col. Rex Applegate.

and has become my standard "flight knife." It's well under the Federal Aviation Administration's (FAA's) 4-inch length limit, but if it gets confiscated by airport security for violating one of their other ever-changing policies (the current bug up their posteriors are serrated edges—oooooh—so mean looking!) it can be replaced economically. I'm not too sure what goes through the minds of the policy makers at the FAA, but I don't know of any terrorists who currently hijack planes with any knife, regardless of size or design. Hijackers have pretty much shown a preference for guns, hand grenades, and other explosives over pocketknives. Which brings us to the real reason defense-minded passengers carry knives when they fly, and it is certainly not to pull them on a bunch of guys with beards, wild eyes, and foreign accents who are pointing AK-47s at you. A far better strategy in such a situation would be to slip that 3-inch Spyderco as far down into your underwear as you can get it, then hope they don't find it and realize you're not just another of the docile bleating sheep they intend to use as bargaining chattel. Then you can wait and watch, and who knows? An opportunity for some reasonable plan of action might eventually present itself.

No, the wise warrior doesn't carry a knife onto an airplane anticipating trouble while onboard; that's not very likely, and if it comes it will be a job for a counterterrorist team, not you and your pocketknife. Those who carry defensive folders when flying do so because they know that travelers are a high-risk group, and they don't care to be mugged, robbed, or raped while they're getting their luggage or trying to hail a cab.

Quality custom-made folders, due to the amount of labor required, are more expensive than custom fixed blades. But if you get exactly what you want, it's worth the extra money. Some of my favorite custom foldermakers are Pat Crawford, Chris Reeves, William W. Harsey, Frank Centofante, Newt Livesay, Ken Onion, and Bob Lum. For you fans of Bob Taylor's nasty little fixed-blade Hobbit, Round Eye Knife and Tool has now come out with a folding version along the same lines. Round Eye is also making Bram Frank's revolutionary new design, the Escalator. Check into Laci Szabo's creations made by a variety of makers, including Black Cloud Knives. There are many other makers grinding out great folding fighters these days, too, and by the time you read this there will be even more. If you want to keep up on the ever-changing market, I'd recommend reading *Tactical Knives* magazine and subscribing to *Modern Knife*, Combat Technologies' new online magazine (www.combattech.com).

BLADE STYLES

Let me say a few words about my preferences in blade styles, and if you don't agree you're welcome to tear this page out of the book and go on. (Some of it is, admittedly, personal preference that borders on prejudice.) I am not a big fan of the tanto point, and I particularly detest chisel-ground blades. (My Newt Livesay Woo knives, while tanto-tipped, are specially made flat-ground models rather than the standard chisel grind.) In fact, I am convinced knife makers and manufacturers came up with the whole chisel-grind fad simply because it meant less work (they only have to grind one side) and it was a good marketing gimmick. (You bet I'd do the same if I were in that business.) Tanto points are as indestructible as you can get—you can indeed drive the quality ones through car hoods and the like. But I have never faced a man whose chest was as tough as a car hood, nor one using a car hood as a shield. Tanto points will also penetrate softer substance (such as human tissue) but not quite as easily as other designs. (Okay, in reality you probably wouldn't even notice the difference in the heat of battle; I warned you I had my own preferences and prejudices.) As for chisel grinds, I can never cut as well with them as I can with a flat or hollow-ground blade, and I find them harder to resharpen. I experience pretty much the same frustration trying to resharpen serrated edges—the serrations do aid some in cutting when they're sharp, but they're lots of work to keep that way, and when I'm finished, I'm never, ever, satisfied with the results.

KNIFE CARRY

Choosing a method of knife carry is as personal as choosing how to carry your gun. There are only two hard-and-fast rules: if you are also carrying a gun, make sure the knife does not interfere with getting to it as quickly as possible, and if the knife is to be your primary weapon, carry it in the most readily accessible place. Even if it's called a "boot knife" it should never go into your boot unless it's part of a multiweapon defense strategy and its role is that of a last-ditch hideout. After that, you're on your own. Belt carry—inside or outside the pants—shoulder rig, up your sleeve, down your back, across your back, you be the judge. Just make sure you can get to it quickly if you need it, because if you need it, you will need it quick.

One of my favorite carries is the neck knife. I find that in this mode I can easily conceal most knives with up to 4-inch blades, and even longer blades of the push-dagger design, such as Cold Steel's Safekeeper I. The only time I don't have a knife suspended around

Weapons are the great equalizer. Here, a young woman with a Newt Livesay neck knife neutralizes an attacker who outweighs her by more than 100 pounds.

my neck is when I'm wearing a pullover shirt tucked in. T-shirts, sweatshirts, or sweaters worn outside the pants make a perfect covering for the neck knife, and even with a button-up shirt the buttons can be ripped away in an emergency. (Find a phone booth first, and tell Lois Lane hello for me when you see her.) If you wear a tie, you can run the cord or chain out through your shirt and down through the loop that holds the tie's small end. I know many uniformed cops who do this. Hanging in my closet I currently have neck knives made by Pat Crawford, Black Cloud, Cold Steel, and Newt Livesay. Livesay, doing business as Wicked Knife Company, makes an entire line of shockingly economical custom fixed blades and has plans for folders on the drawing board. Perhaps his hottest seller at the moment is the Woo neck knife I already mentioned, a 3-inch chisel-ground tanto. Around my neck while I am typing this, I am wearing what I call my Woo-Woo—two Woos whose custom sheaths screw together to become one unit. They can also be worn separately.

LEGAL CONSIDERATIONS

Just like any weapon you carry and might have to use, you should always be aware of your local laws. Then, if you decide for whatever reason to violate them, you at least know what you're up against. Here in Oklahoma, it is generally legal to carry, openly or concealed, any folder regardless of length. Fixed blades, however, regardless of size, are technically illegal. But the statutes include exemption for sporting and recreational purposes. Wise knife-carriers, therefore, do not even own any "defensive" knives. Even their bowies and daggers are recreational blades (practicing self-defense is one of your hobbies, isn't it?), and in addition to the knife, they carry a "story" to go with it. Get my drift?

But like every other state with which I am acquainted, Oklahoma has a "catch all" statute that basically says nothing may be carried with the intent of doing physical harm to anyone. This means that if you have a Swiss Army Knife and there is evidence that you intend to hurt someone with it, you can be arrested. In addition to state laws, there are city ordinances of which you should be aware.

My advice is that most of the time it is wise to stay within the law. If the jurisdiction you live in has a 4-inch blade length limit, you are not giving up too much carrying a knife with a 3 7/8-inch blade. If the limit is 3 inches, go to 2 7/8 inches. In all honesty, there is not too much defensive work that can be performed with a 4-inch blade that can't be done almost equally well with 3 inches. With small blades like either of these, slashing and short, fast thrusts to the face and other critical areas are the name of the game. Not until you get up to at least 5 inches in blade length are you going to go deep enough into the body to consistently reach vital organs.

TRAINING WITH THE DEFENSIVE KNIFE

Even if you personally have no intention of ever carrying a knife, you should at least learn the basics of knife fighting. Why? Because then you stand a better chance of defending yourself against an attacker armed with a blade. More and more good knife-defense programs are being offered, and we'll look at some of them a little later. Right now, keep in mind that once again the KISS rule applies (Keep It Simple, Stupid). Work out some opening move blade strategies of your own, and practice them. This might mean taking the suggestion of some teachers that you cut the first initial of your name. Referring back to the chart in Chapter 4, we see that if I cut the first letter of my last name I would be performing movements number 2, then 1. My only real advice in developing your opening moves is to remember that the vast majority of other people's opening attacks come from between 3:00 and 12:00 on the chart you superimpose over them, and come at you within the 9:00 and 12:00 area. That is, of course, because most attackers, like most people in general, are right-handed, and most people are more familiar with physical movement that follows the 1, 3, and 11 lines. They learned these lines in childhood by learning to throw a ball, swing a baseball bat or tennis racket, and a variety of other activities. So, while we can't assume all opening attacks will be in that area, we can hope that our opponent does. And we can design our own opening counterattack with the odds in mind, which means picking any of the other lines besides these three.

Like any other weapon you plan to stake your life on, training with the knife is essential, and there are several routes to proficiency you can take. Regardless of which you choose, please, first either buy one of the excellent commercial training knives on the market today or make one yourself. Trainers can range from high-quality aluminum reproductions of the specific knife you plan to carry to the one you saw from a piece of scrap plywood. Rubber knives or rolled up newspapers are usually best for sparring and fast two-man drills. But wood or dulled steel can add that little element of pain that induces faster learning, too. Eye protection is a good idea even with soft rubber trainers.

The first and most convenient way for many people to learn the use of the knife is to train themselves. (Remember what Musashi said, however: this opens paths not available through a teacher, but some are false.) Take the 12 planes of motion chart in Chapter 4 and begin learning the slashes, cuts, and thrusts—first in sequence, then out of order, and then in fast two- to five-technique combinations. A good heavy bag is a great training aid after you've learned the movements "in the air." (I'm talking about with a trainer, of course; your bag won't last long with a real blade.) I often use a double-ended striking ball to develop speed and accuracy on a moving target as well. You can make a cutting dummy out of old clothes and wet newspapers to see just how well your blade of choice actually works. At least some time should be spent cutting and thrusting at a tree or another hard surface so you learn what it's like to strike bone and still keep the knife in your hand. You may be surprised at how poorly some of the high-dollar exotic fighting knives actually perform compared to the simple basic blade shapes. At least one training partner, and preferably more than one, will eventually become necessary in order to create a realistic program. Cutting a dummy or practicing against an inanimate punching bag is one thing; doing the same to another person, particularly a wild-eyed slobbering maniac screaming obscenities, is another. You should learn to parry as well as strike, because in the same sense that paper pistol targets don't shoot back, stationary striking bags, balls, posts, or whatever you choose, do not attack you either.

In the 1970s, we used to laugh at people who thought they could learn martial arts solely by reading books on the subject. But if you use books in conjunction with instruction from a teacher, or decide to go Musashi's lone wolf route with a few training partners, books are tremendous aids. The video training tape has taken home training one step further, allowing the student to view techniques from beginning to end and from different angles. Of course if you have a question, there is no teacher to ask. But you can run the tape back and play it over and over through the part you don't understand until you do. If you still don't get it, use your brain. Break the problem down and analyze it and come up with your own solution. It may not end up working as well as the one you missed on the tape, but then again it may work better for you since you were forced to come up with it yourself. Now, let me relate a quick story to illustrate the point I'm trying to get across.

I have never been a very patient person, and I've always had trouble learning things that held no interest for me. Occasionally, however, I find that I must learn something I find tedious in order to move on to something I want to do. When I decided I wanted to become a writer, it became pretty obvious that I would have to learn to type—a skill I had avoided through high school and college by always seeming to have a girlfriend willing to type my essays and reports for me. So at the age of 29 I bought a book on typing and sat down to learn. Boring. Horribly boring. I followed the directions halfway through, got sick of them, and made up the rest. I now have my own style of typing that has been described as looking like someone playing the piano. But it works. And as long as the letter "a" appears on the screen whenever I want it to, I don't see that it makes much difference. Think about this: it applies to learning self-defense as well as typing.

Many traditional martial arts include edged weapons in their curriculum, and others are directly based upon the blade. As I've said before, as long as you're willing to separate the wheat from the chaff and decide which techniques are applicable to today's society and which would have been better left in the rural areas of 17th-century Hokkaido, this is not a bad way to learn. The Chinese have their swords, daggers, and knives; the Japanese practice ken-jitsu, tanto-jitsu, and other arts. The dagger and knife have long been the favorite backup weapons for the older European sword arts. The knife training found in Filipino kali, escrima, and arnis, with their practice of *espada* (sword) and *daga* (dagger or knife) and the art of espada y daga (the sword and knife in conjunction) is perhaps the most directly applicable to today's streets. Many of the techniques used with the bowie knife are modified versions of saber fencing movements, so if you find out that your next-door neighbor is a fencing maestro, you might want to borrow a cup of sugar now and then. Military knife training is usually directed more at silently taking out sentries and similar tasks, but some of it bears at least a passing resemblance to street defense. So if you find someone willing to teach you, or want to learn such techniques through videotapes or whatever, go for it— it can't hurt. There's no such thing as too much knowledge, but don't expect everything you learn to apply directly to self-defense.

The best way to study the knife is to hook up with one of the new schools of American defense I mentioned earlier. They cut directly to the bone (okay, bad pun, but they can't all be gems) and teach today's defense with today's weapons. But I've devoted a whole chapter later to such schools, and it's time to move on to stick defense. So let's get crackin'.

The sword is the protector of all.

—Seneca
Hercules Furens, c. 50

7

Canes, Umbrellas, and Other Impact Weapons

Sticks and Stones May Break My Bones

Turning to the men, Musashi told them to find weapons.
"Anything will do, even a good heavy stick or a length of fresh
bamboo."

—Eiji Yoshikawa
Musashi, 1971

Well, it was a toss-up this time whether to open this chapter with the above words from the novel that has become known as the *Gone with the Wind* of Japan or to quote the more famous words of my favorite president, Theodore Roosevelt: "Speak softly and carry a big stick." But I figured you were probably already familiar with Teddy's advice. In any case, the sentiments expressed by both Roosevelt and Yoshikawa support one of the main points of this chapter: the modest stick is one of the—if not *the*—oldest weapon known to man, and it is still an excellent self-defense item in today's world—sometimes the best choice of all.

It's impossible to determine exactly what man's first weapon was. But somewhere in early human history, about the same time it occurred to one of our grunting hirsute ancestors that a rock made a less painful hammer than his hand, he likely also figured out that it made more sense to hit his enemies over the head with something that wasn't as filled with fragile bones and nerve centers as his hand. This "something" may well have been another rock, but it might just as easily have been a fallen tree branch. Yes, the stick as weapon has been with us for a long time, and it is no less functional for modern self-defense than it was in the days when men called themselves names like Zork.

Just like the rock, the stick was, and is, an impact weapon. And the first time Zork picked up a long one, swung it at another caveman, and said to himself, "Ugh! Stick good! Help me stay away at same time I hit!" the extension weapon was also born.

Fighting sticks are everywhere around us, but being the masters of disguise that they are, they camouflage themselves. Even as you read this, one is standing against the wall of your laundry room trying to pass itself off as a broom. Another is lying on the floor in the hall closet telling you it's actually a vacuum cleaner extension, and your garage is absolutely infested with these imposters masquerading as hoes, shovels, and rakes. Do not be fooled! These guys are fighters! They may actually do a little work around the house sometimes to foster their cover identities, but what they're really there for is to save your life someday.

Refer back to the 12 planes of motion chart in Chapter 4. The same rules of movement that applied to knives pertain to sticks. There are a few minor differences in what the stick does, but they do not involve the actual physics of the overall movements. You can slash, stab, and thrust with sticks just like you would with an edged weapon. These can be large follow-through blows or short snapping strikes, so *witik* and *lobtik* your little hearts out. Of course, the barrel of a stick will not cut deeply into the flesh like an edged weapon, and the end of a blunt stick will not penetrate like a stiletto or ice pick. But they still concentrate great amounts of energy into small striking areas and prove very effective in their own way. If you don't believe me, fasten a broom handle horizontally into that vice on your workbench. Now move to the opposite wall, lower your head, and sprint into the end of the broom handle as hard as you can. When you wake up, you'll be convinced. While the stick will not actually cut or stab (although the skin may indeed be broken, resulting in an abrasion), it has a couple of advantages over edged weapons that help to make up for that deficiency.

First, the stick allows for a wider margin of error in the execution of technique. When you swing a knife or sword, you must take some pains to ensure that the edge is in line with your target. With a stick, this does not apply. And while the rolling motion so stressed in Japanese stick arts like *bo* and *jo* (6-foot and 4-foot staffs, respectively) is helpful, it is not essential to success any more than failure to execute the twist in a karate or tae kwon do punch will render it completely useless. The stick is also appropriate at many different threat levels—from that brother-in-law we keep talking about all the way to, and through, the armed assailant who threatens your very life.

Unless you are a professional landscaper or have some similar occupation that demands it, I suspect few of you carry a hoe, shovel, broom, or similar tool-stick-weapon with you when you leave the house. So if you choose the stick as a means of street self-defense, it must blend into today's society in order to avoid drawing attention. That usually means a walking stick of some sort, or possibly an umbrella. There are minor disparities in the techniques that are applicable to each due to the differences in length. But a good many of the basics are the same, and with a little practice and thought you will easily be able to determine what works better with long sticks and what should be reserved for the shorter impact weapons.

The walking stick, or cane, is one of my favorite defensive items. I had practiced with them some already but didn't truly discover their utility until a few years ago while recovering from back surgery. Yes, necessity *is* the mother of invention. During the first few weeks out of the hospital, I found that while walking was not a problem, getting up and sitting down always threatened to bring some very unmasculine tears to my eyes. I purchased a simple wooden cane at a drugstore, and, being who I am, just had to discover its potential as a weapon. I think I hit my water-filled heavy bag twice before it snapped in two. So I was off to the lumberyard, and when I got back

I had a new shovel handle with me. A trip to Hobby Lobby (I can't believe I admitted that in print) and another stop at the drugstore, and I'd procured a round wooden ball and a rubber crutch tip. The wooden ball fit well in the palm of my hand and made a good grip, and the crutch tip, with a little stretching, fit the end of the shovel handle. After that, it was simply a matter of cutting the stick to proper length and attaching the wooden ball with a double-threaded screw. (I knew that seventh-grade shop class would prove handy someday.) I now had a big, thick, sturdy, baseball-bat-like bone-breaker walking stick that wasn't going to fly into pieces if I had to defend myself. The ball grip and crutch tip pretty much balanced each other on the ends. The barrel was slightly larger around than a typical police baton but could be used like one quite well. I begin to adapt many of the two-handed *jo* and *bo* techniques I had practiced over the years, grip changes and all. I was happy.

Then I got to wondering what I'd do if one of my hands was busy fending off an attacker who had entered my danger zone before I could react, or was occupied with some other task when the time for action came. The heavy shovel-cane could be used one-handed but was clumsy in that mode. It wouldn't be useless by any means, but it was slower than I wanted. I had an old *jo* that had broken during training, so I sawed it off, returned to Hobby Lobby and the drugstore, and made a new, lighter walking stick. But I still was not satisfied.

The crux of the problem was the fact that the most important technique in any self-defense encounter is almost always the *first* one. And that initial strike rarely comes after you've taken a "fighting stance." Assuming that you are walking, or standing, or even seated with the grip of your walking stick in your hand and the tip on the ground, the fastest opening movement is a number 12 (on the chart) delivered to the groin, knee, or other available target area. All other strikes from this position require you to first reposition the stick, which takes time you probably do not have. Now, even my shovel-cane could be moved upward fairly fast if I used both hands, and the *jo*-cane even moved with reasonable speed one-handed. But this movement, in its purest and fastest form, starts with the cane in a static position and must be accomplished with nothing more than a flip of the wrist. Unless you have Arnold Schwarzenegger's forearms, this cannot be done speedily with a heavy stick. And even Arnold could do it faster with a lighter cane than he could a heavy one.

I found the answer, or at least the first part of the answer, to my problem in the Cold Steel Special Projects catalog. Cold Steel, in addition to its excellent line of knives, imports several lengths of the Indian Police Lahti, which is used by officers in India in the same role as our own riot baton. Constructed of rattan instead of hardwood, however, it is considerably lighter. I bought one of the shorter 4-foot versions (standard Indian police issue), but it was still longer than I wanted. You see, you can walk down most any street in America with a cane, particularly if you are over 30 years old, and people will say, "There goes an old man with a cane." But carry anything as long as a hiking or camping staff, and they say, "There goes a man with a club." By now, however, my cross saw practically knew what to do on its own. Thirty minutes later I had a tough, lightweight defense weapon who had joined his stick brothers in deception and was swearing to the world, "I'm just here to help the poor old guy get around."

That's probably the number-one advantage of the cane or walking stick as a weapon. Not only is it effective, it's *so* politically correct. I mean, what kind of low-life scumbag monster picks on a poor defenseless man or woman who has to walk with a cane? The only better weapon in this respect would be one that screamed, "Please! We must do it to save the children!" Buy or make a cane out of anything you want—rattan, wood, aluminum, steel, or even hard plastic. You can carry it anywhere, and no one will give you a second look. Of course, if you're 20 years old and wearing a University of Nebraska football letter jacket instead of 46 and sporting a white beard and receding hairline like me, you might want to learn to limp a little when you near the airport security checkpoint. (Tell them it came from a knee injury in the Kansas State game.) But just keep playing football, and by the time you reach my age the limp will come naturally.

Short story along those lines: I went through an airport security check in Seattle, Washington, a few years ago, making a flight connection that would eventually lead to my first Combat Technology Riddle of Steel knife/counterknife seminar in Hell's Canyon. I was carrying a very beautiful and well-made cane made by Eric Sporthauer called the Urban Walker, which has a side handle and looks like a longer version of the Okinawan tonfa or the police PR-24 baton. I had barely taken my seat when a face I'd never seen before sat down next to me and began talking about the Riddle. He turned out to be Dr. Mike Kay, a psychologist and martial artist from Pennsylvania who had already attended the biyearly training seminar several times in the past. When I asked him how he knew where I was going, he grinned and told me I'd quit limping as soon as I was out of sight of the security check. Oh, well. The ability to work undercover is like any other skill; you don't use it for awhile, you lose it.

When you buy or make your cane, there are a few things to keep in mind. First, you have to balance weight with the ability to do damage. I mean, a cane made out of cardboard would be even faster than one made out of rattan, wouldn't it? But it wouldn't do much more than really irritate an attacker, no matter where you hit him. Even with a light rattan stick, you're going to have to pick your targets to a certain extent. A solid strike across the thigh with a rattan stick will sting like a whole hive of bees and discourage many assailants—but not all of them. A stick with only reasonable weight will break a collarbone, however, and that will take care of the next level of attacker. If you are unlucky enough to be chosen as a potential victim by one of the mentally ill, methamphetamine- or crack-crazed kamikaze aggressors haunting our streets today, you may well find that he does not cease and desist until you've rendered him unconscious, broken both legs so badly he can't stand up, or taken his life.

Don't ever mistakenly believe that all blows to the head with a stick will take a man out of action. I once watched a guy who must have weighed 220 pounds break the heavy end of a pool cue over the head of a man who probably tipped the scales at 150. The little guy went down—for about a second and a half. They next thing we knew, about a half-dozen of us had to pull him off the big guy to keep the big guy from getting killed. God designed the skull like a helmet to protect the brain, and it is thick in most places. The temples, and a few other areas, are the exceptions that He threw in so we "good guys" would stand a fighting chance against the animals. But they aren't always easy to access during the heat of battle.

We spoke of "defanging the snake" in the chapter about knives, but it should be reemphasized here. An opponent's weapon must be your primary concern, so if he's holding a gun or knife or his own stick or any other weapon, render it useless first. Then, if the threat persists, attack the man who is still attacking you.

Let's look for a moment at the different types of canes available today. Although there are minor variations of both, the two primary types of canes are the straight walking stick and the crook top. Either can be employed as a striking instrument and used as a lever in certain traps, joint locks, sweeps, and throws. The crook top adds an additional dimension with its hooking features. Pull the hook up into your opponent's groin, grasp a handful of his hair, and his heart and soul will soon follow. This is just one of literally dozens of techniques too numerous to go into here. If you want a really good education in the use of the crook handle cane, I recommend John Pelligrini's two-volume video set, *The Hapkido Cane*. John goes well beyond anything you are ever likely to need in self-defense, but that's what good learning is all about. It's always better to know too much than too little. *The Hapkido Cane* is well produced, and the opera soundtrack is a delightful change from the hard rock we usually get with self-defense videos today.

The sword cane offers another new dimension. It can be used as a regular cane, or the blade can be drawn. Most sword cane blades are not actually long enough to be called true swords; rather, they are long knives. But if you train yourself to draw the blade quickly, you then have a weapon in both hands, and you can employ the same techniques used with the European sword and dagger, the Filipino espada y daga, or, to a certain extent, any of the other two-handed weapon disciplines. Having a weapon in both hands as a means of defense is truly baffling to an assailant unaccustomed to such counterattacks. The weapon-in-both-hands school of thought is the best example I've ever seen of Kurt Lewin's theory of synergy: the sum of the parts is greater than the whole. The same effect, in varying degrees of lethality, can be achieved with a regular cane and a knife carried separately, or a pair of knives, or a weapon in just one hand and the recognition that you haven't lost your other fist.

The primary problem with the sword cane is that it's illegal to carry in every place of which I am aware. Don't try sneaking one through airport security; they X-ray canes just like they do carry-on bags. Even if they don't, the steel of the blade is going to set off the metal detector's alarm. The other negative to the sword cane is its cost; good ones are expensive. Yeah, I know you can get the ones out of the catalog for $19.95, but you get what you pay for. Walk with one for a couple of days and you'll find the latching mechanism broken just from tapping it along the ground. If the idea of a sword cane trips your trigger, you're going to have to shell out the bucks. I have an excellent one made by Pat Crawford, which is actually part of his modular survival staff. The components of this staff can be broken down, transforming it from a long hiking staff to a cane and on to a swagger stick if so desired. Each section will hide the blade, and the aluminum shaft is a wicked little stick all on its own.

I am very fond of the Urban Walker cane I mentioned earlier, made by Eric Sporthauer. It's a heavy bone-crusher. But unless you have sufficient room to take advantage of the torque available by swinging it by the side-handle (another finishing blow), it's a two-handed weapon. For you martial artists who have trained with the tonfa, or police officers who are well versed with the PR-24, it's an excellent choice. Of course it looks considerably different from a normal cane, and I suspect that in addition to the fact my limp was not consistent, that was another thing that tipped off my friend Mike Kay. Still, I have never had anyone question the Urban Walker when I've carried it.

As to training with a cane or other stick, it's like the knife—there are several viable methods. You can again take the 12 planes of motion chart and begin learning to move along them with strikes and thrusts. I'd recommend practicing the movements first in sequence,

While firearms are the best overall method of self-defense, they are not always available or practical. In this photo, a potential victim repels an attacker armed with a baseball bat by using one of Pat Crawford's excellent sword canes.

then out of sequence, and then putting together combinations. You can use the same heavy bag, and you can even use the same cane or other stick instead of a trainer. The double-end striking ball once more comes in handy to develop speed and accuracy, and you'll eventually want training partners for more reality.

If you choose to go the traditional route, the same warnings I gave you for the knife apply to the stick. The Okinawan styles are famous for their use of the *bo, sai*, and nunchaku. Aikido relies heavily on the *jo* as both a training aid to teach concepts and as a weapon in and of itself. The Chinese arts have their sticks, and the Koreans use the cane extensively. In addition to swords, our European ancestors practiced with maces, war hammers, quarter staves, and a variety of other clubs. Every ancient society in history developed impact weapons of one sort or another, and once in awhile you find someone teaching some of the more uncommon disciplines in a school or his garage or backyard. Some of them are worth checking into.

Again, as with the knife, some of the very best stick training around comes to us from the Philippines. Another advantage found with the Filipino arts is that they begin teaching weapons almost immediately rather than first requiring the student to reach a relatively high level of unarmed skill. The commonly used *baston* (about 24 inches) is considerably shorter than the average cane but translates quite well to the umbrella. At 32 inches, the *yantok* is still shorter than the walking stick of the average man, but not so much so that the techniques cannot be adapted easily.

Once again, however, I must voice my opinion that one of the modern American schools of self-defense is your best direct route to combat success. You will not put on a gi and practice stick fighting with sticks you never see outside of a dojo or martial arts supply store. You'll train with the cane, the umbrella, the pool cue, and other impact weapons common to today's world. Should you be lucky enough to live within reasonable distance of one of the programs we look at later on in this book or another system that fits the bill, "get thee to that nunnery" immediately! If this isn't practical, many of these instructors tour the United States conducting seminars every year. Again, *Tactical Knives*, *Modern Knife* (online), and most of the martial arts and gun magazines carry ads that include schedules for such training sessions. In addition to what they teach, the modern instructors who lead these seminars will encourage self-education and individual thought on your part. They won't spoon-feed you or tell you their way is the only way. If they do, beware. You're not dealing with a modern self-defense instructor but another of the "gurus" who has simply hidden his gi and disguised himself in a sweat suit, jeans, or combat fatigues.

I've already stressed the importance I place on the quick draw of the gun, and we've looked at the old cop adage, "The fastest draw is already having the gun in your hand." The same applies to any weapon, and a cane and umbrella are always in your hand. There is simply no substitute for quick access of your defense medium when unexpected trouble comes your way.

But neither the cane nor the umbrella is the ideal everyday carry weapon for everyone. I feel comfortable with a walking stick in my hand today, at my age, but in my younger years that would not have been the case. And even today, you wouldn't catch me dead carrying an umbrella on my way to a dogfight in a thunderstorm. As with every other weapon, if you feel the daily carry of an impact weapon is for you, you must pick one that suits your personal life-style. And whether you intend to carry a stick with you or not, learn to use one. You never know when that broom in your closet might suddenly jump into your hands and reveal its true identity.

A stick in the hand is better than a tongue in the mouth.
—Yiddish Proverb

8

Nonlethal Weapons and the Overall Defense Package

Keep the Pepper Spray Out of *Your* Face

All the armed prophets conquered; all the unarmed ones perished.

—Niccolo Machiavelli
The Prince, VI, 1513

You've got to love old Machiavelli. He gets straight to the point.

Quick review: Man without gun must be lucky, man with gun stupid (Toguchi); there are no drive-by kickings (Keating); 1 determined 12-year-old + 1 pocketknife = 12 years in a gi (VanCook).

What's that tell us, boys and girls? A determined attitude combined with some kind of weapon is better than all the training in the world. Some weapons are better than others, but in the same sense that a .22 in your hand is worth more than the .44 at home in your dresser drawer, any weapon is better than no weapon at all. Now, one more quick reminder before we get into this chapter (Machiavelli brings it up inadvertently by speaking of prophets): beware the false prophets selling their feel-good-about-yourself-and-don't-hurt-anybody self-defense programs. Worthless gadgets and gizmos are among their specialties. Taking advantage once again of good people's aversion to hurting others, these shysters present their contraptions to the good-hearted-but-naive public with the promise that they will get you out of danger without your having to hurt your assailant. (Set phasors to stun, Mr. Spock!) These snake oil salesmen are in business to make money, period, and one way they do that is by selling ineffectual toys to accompany their impotent programs. I can't stress this enough: you and I live in a real world, not one of those old herbal shampoo commercials where cute little talking cartoon animals float peacefully down the stream in a boat, happy birds chirp in the trees overhead, and everyone loves everyone else. We live in a world where there are talking animals all right, but instead of love, peace, and understanding, they concentrate on rape, murder, and robbery. If they decide to hurt you, you are more than likely going to have to hurt *them* to keep that from happening. If they want to kill you, it's just like Colonel Applegate said in the title of his book—"kill or get killed." Yes, it's too bad. But there is simply no other way.

Once again, however, we must understand that not every self-defense situation is a matter of life or death; there are many different levels of threat. Therefore, some of the items we usually refer to as nonlethal definitely have a place in the personal protection battery. Are you going to blow your drunken brother-in-law's head off with a 12-gauge shotgun? Thrust the 7 1/2-inch blade of your Cold Steel Tai-Pan dagger through the heart of the date who tries one more time to kiss you after you've said "no"? Of course not. Shooting or cutting someone would not be necessary or morally justified in such scenarios. But that doesn't mean you don't have a problem, and to solve such problems, chemical sprays or other nonlethal items may be exactly the level of force you need.

There is a multitude of these items on the market today, and we'll look at some of the better ones in a moment. First, it's important to understand that the only ones you should put any faith in are those of the chemical spray or impact weapon variety. Even these must be considered realistically; their role in your self-defense battery must be accurately identified and not exaggerated. In other words, don't make the mistake of thinking they're the solution to a life-threatening situation, and don't count on them to always be effective against even lesser threats. Like any other weapons, they can malfunction, be dropped, or be knocked from the hand. Their role is in handling less-than-lethal situations and serving as backup to other weapons.

What you actually need is not a weapon but a weapons system, which includes verbal reasoning, unarmed combat, less-than-lethal weapons, and deadly weapons. If there is time, and an attacker can be talked out of his attack, great. Keep in mind, however, that what begins as a mere nuisance can quickly escalate into a more serious threat. You may have about one-tenth of a second to go from the verbal reasoning stage to a defense that will determine whether you live or die. Correctly identifying the level of threat, then choosing the appropriate weapon and response, is usually the trickiest part of self-defense. Choosing tactics that later appear to have been too deadly for the situation can land you in jail. Tactics not deadly enough will get you killed. One rule of thumb to keep in mind is that nonlethal weapons are usually only effective on attackers who planned to stop at a certain point anyway. They will rarely end the aggressions of a determined rapist or murderer.

Let's look at the popular pepper sprays and see exactly what they can and can't do. Made of oleoresin capsicum, they were touted as the perfect less-than-lethal way to combat violence when they first came out a few years ago. The bottom line? They are a dramatic improvement over the tear gas (actually a form of CS/CN riot control agent) they replaced, but no, they haven't proven to be the magic elixir their manufacturers advertised them to be. They are not always effective, any more than anything else is always effective. Police now have many documented cases of drugged-out zombies and other madmen who, after they were finally overpowered in other ways, did little more than complain that the pepper spray used during the arrest had burned their eyes a little.

Pepper sprays usually come in either 5- or 10-percent solutions. Get the 10-percent. It still won't be enough to stop the crack addict willing to rob and kill you for his next smoke, but it will definitely discourage sane attackers. Outdoors, be sure you are upwind. Inside, figure ahead of time that you are going to get at least a little of the spray in your own eyes and be mentally prepared for the pain. In either case, as soon as you've shot a liberal dose into your attacker's face, employ another weapon if the situation calls for it or get out of there as fast as you can.

A friend of mine, a local policeman, wouldn't use this stuff again if his life depended on it. Several years ago, shortly after undergoing pepper-spray training (yes, today's politically correct police administrators think officers need a class on button-pressing . . . duh?), he found himself chasing a fleeing felon down an alley. Drawing to within a pace or so of the subject, he whipped out his trusty canister and fogged the area just beyond the running man. He misjudged slightly, and the suspect ran past the cloud before the mist could settle in the air. The officer, however, timed it perfectly, and ran headfirst into the fog. He wound up sitting next to a trashcan for half an hour with his gun out, blindly sputtering, "Don't come close or I'll shoot!" The suspect hasn't been heard from since.

The bottom line: keep the role of pepper sprays and other defensive gases in perspective. They are for use in low-level threat situations and should be considered augmentations, not replacements, for other weapons.

Personally, I place more faith in nonlethal impact weapons. The *kubotan* is one example. Based on the Japanese *yawara* stick and sometimes called a fist load, the *kubotan* is nothing more than a stick slightly longer than the width of the palm. This leaves a hard end sticking out on both sides of the hand and allows for both forehand and backhand strikes. It can also be applied to nerve centers to assist in come-alongs and restraint techniques. It, too, is often classified as a "nonlethal" weapon, and certainly it can be used as such. On the other hand, hard blows to the temple, throat, and other areas with the *kubotan* can cause death. Of course, if you spray someone with enough pepper spray, mace, or anything else, they'll die, too.

A favorite nonlethal impact weapon of mine is the COMTECH Stinger, a punching device made of injection-molded plastic that works similarly to a push dagger. The base of the Stinger fits into the palm of the hand, and the "nose" extends between the index and middle fingers. This allows a tremendous amount of force to be concentrated on a relatively small area, and even a weaker person's punches take on the knockout capacity of George Foreman. Like the *yawara*-based striking devices, the Stinger can be used against arms, legs, and ribs in less-than-deadly confrontations and to the face and throat when it's for all the marbles. I've done several demonstrations with these handy little devices, and a mere snapping motion of the wrist splits 1-inch pine boards.

Another one, the DTL (which stands for Destroy, Trap, and Lock) Impact Kerambit, is somewhat new to me, but I'm very impressed with what I've been able to make it do so far. With an integral finger ring at one end and several holes spaced throughout its L-shaped configuration, it looks more like a plastic wrench from some complicated toy you bought your kid last Christmas than a weapon. Like the Stinger, it concentrates the force of a blow onto a small area. For the more advanced martial artist, it's also designed for blocking, trapping limbs, employing restraint tactics, and pressing into nerve centers. Both the Stinger and DTL have an added advantage over the *yawara*: they allow the user to retain partial dexterity of the hand for grabbing, pulling, and so on without losing the weapon.

One advantage of most of the small impact weapons is that they are conveniently carried—often on a key chain. This means you can have them in your hand and draw little or no attention, whereas a gun or knife would likely bring screams from everyone you passed on the sidewalk. Walking through a darkened underground parking garage at night, you appear to be just a man or woman carrying a key ring, which is perfectly logical and normal in this setting. Yet you have a weapon in your hand and ready, and fumbling the draw under the stress of attack is no longer an issue. (The same thing can be achieved with small folding knives carried closed in the hand.)

All through this text I've made sarcastic remarks about the people who extol the cellular phone as the end-all solution to violence. But I've also said that, kept in perspective, cellular phones do have a place in self-defense. Okay, if you should find yourself in a threatening situation or are confronted with an attacker, in the unlikely event that you have enough time and are in a position to do so, tap in 911 on your trusty cell phone and call the police. I see no reason to stop the sarcasm now, however, so unless you're prepared to take charge of your own welfare between the time of the call and the time the squad car arrives, you'd better try one of those "goodness and light" aura things in surround sound. Here's a more practical way you could use your phone: strike your assailant over the head with it 10 or 15 times, or until you're sure he's not going to attack again. Most cellular phones are made of hard plastic and will stand up to it. Then you can call the cops again and find out what's taking them so long to get there.

The same can be said about some of the ink-spray "mark your attacker" gadgets, and the "loud noise" devices that are supposed to draw attention your way and scare off assailants. They aren't the best clubs around, but they'll serve in a pinch. There's even a practical use for those whistles that are supposed to summon help as dependably as Jimmy Olson's wrist radio calls Superman: if you've trained with flexible weapons and can get the chain or lanyard off your neck before the attacker uses it to strangle you, they make pretty decent whips.

Among the most overlooked means of defense today are modern hand tools. I had an experience several years ago that left me with my mouth hanging open. I was in an outdoor sporting goods store when a guy walked in and began looking at folding knives. He looked like he'd just come in off a construction job, as he had on one of those leather tool belts that look like Old West *buscadero* rigs but carry hammers, screwdrivers, and pliers instead of six-guns and cartridge loops. The belt reminded me of Harpo's coat in one of the old Marx Brothers movies—if Groucho or Chico had asked this guy for a fish I'm sure he could have found one in there somewhere. Anyway, during the course of his conversation with the salesman, I overheard him say that his wife's ex-husband had been around causing trouble. The guy with a whole toolbox hanging from his hips was looking for a weapon to defend himself if the need arose. He ended up buying a cheap Pakistani steel folding knife that wasn't sharp, couldn't be sharpened, and wouldn't have made as effective a weapon as any of two-dozen things he already had in his tool belt.

Think of the American Indian's tomahawk. Now think of the modern claw hammer. Think of the Italian stiletto. Now think of a screwdriver. Picture the Viking's battle axe and then the hatchet you use to chop kindling for your fireplace, and the Filipino *baston* and then the tire tool in the trunk of your car. Now, go back to the 12 planes of motion chart. Set down your knives and sticks, and pick up the claw hammer. Get my drift? Like sticks, other weapons are masters of disguise and just love to try to convince you they're really tools.

There is another reason to incorporate tools into your warrior mind-set today. History has proven, over and over, that oppressive governments, be they foreign or domestic, do their best to disarm the populace they wish to control. The Japanese did it to the Okinawans, the Spanish did it to the Filipinos, and the Nazis did it first to the Jews and then to the rest of the Germans. It's always done under the banner of "law and order," but the true purpose is to make sure that citizens can't fight back against a dictatorial government.

Right now, the United States of America, little by little, is doing this very thing to you and me. The more oppressive our government gets, the more frightened our leaders become of an armed citizenry. You see, they watched what happened in all the Eastern Bloc countries in the late 1980s and 1990s, and finally to the Soviet Union itself. They know that sooner or later, when the common man has had enough, he strikes back. No, I am not advocating an armed revolution. The time for that has not yet come, and I seriously doubt that I'll live to see it when it does come. What we are living in now is a sort of purgatory in which we aren't nearly as free as we used to be, but it's not quite bad enough to tear things down and start over. This leaves us in a state wherein it is often wise to be armed but not appear to be armed. Let's look at why that's so.

I grew up in Enid, a city of 50,000 people in northern Oklahoma. When I was around twelve years old, it was common practice for my friends and me to strap our .22 rifles to the handlebars of our bicycles, ride through residential areas and out into the country, find an open space with a safe backdrop, and spend Saturday afternoons shooting. When we passed police cars on our way out of the city, we waved and they waved back. Once we were popping off rounds in the boonies, an occasional deputy sheriff or state trooper might even stop and give us a few pointers. One even let me shoot his .357 magnum—the first one I'd ever seen.

Except in a very few select rural areas in this country, days like that are over. What do you think the reaction of a police officer today would be if he saw four or five 12-year-olds peddling along the streets of a city with rifles? He's not going to wave and drive on by, I can promise you that. No, today's cop takes a very different position. This is sad, but I can't blame the boys in blue; it's a different world today. You see, when I was 12 years old I also recall riding my bicycle all the way across town to see the house where a murder had taken place the night before. It was the first murder Enid police had dealt with in almost 10 years, and it had all 50,000 people talking.

Today, Enid averages half a dozen murders per year. That's roughly a 6,000 percent increase in the murder rate since I was a kid, and rape, robbery, and other violent crimes have followed suit. Enid is hardly unique in this violent crime rate increase, and it has affected the way police look at anyone who has a weapon.

Do not misinterpret that last sentence. It means there is a difference in how a police officer will approach you if you are armed today compared to how he would have approached you 30 years ago. (He's got to protect himself, you know.) It does not mean that most police officers are against your having guns or other self-defense weapons. In spite of what the liberal media and unscrupulous gun-grabbers like Sarah Brady would have you believe (yes, I feel sorry for her husband—especially every time she wheels him on stage to exploit his condition for her own personal benefit), the vast majority of cops support your right to keep and bear arms. Newspapers and television commentators who use law enforcement agency heads to apparently contradict this are quoting carefully chosen minions who have become politicians rather than cops. All studies indicate that the vast majority of the *real* police officers are staunchly against gun control.

I've already advised you to get a concealed carry permit if you qualify. But I've also reminded you there will still be times you can't legally carry your gun. You can always be armed in one way or another, however, if you learn to use tools and other common everyday items as weapons. We've talked about hammers and screwdrivers and the like, but we aren't limited to these things. Use your imagination. Get a list of everything that's considered contraband in jails and prisons and you'll have an excellent catalog of weapons of opportunity from masters of violence. You see, most prisoners have nothing to do all day but lift weights, file frivolous lawsuits, rape each other, and sit around thinking up new ways of hurting people. Take advantage of their time and effort but put their research to good use.

My wife teases me that before I buy anything—even a new shirt—I evaluate its potential as a weapon. She's right. I don't do this consciously, but I know I do it. I know that a ballpoint pen or sharp pencil makes an excellent thrusting device to soft areas of the body, and that the spine of a book across the throat of an attacker can cause death. Learn to think of—and how to use—everyday items as weapons. The Okinawans did this when the Japanese refused to allow them to own swords; the nunchaku is actually a rice flail. The *bo* was a long staff used to carry two buckets of water suspended across the shoulders. The *kama* was a sickle used in harvest. In fact all of the "traditional" weapons of Okinawan karate are farm implements or tools of one sort or another. The Japanese allowed the Okinawans to keep them because the economy would have collapsed if they didn't. So the oppressed people learned to fight with what they had.

Picture yourself stopped for a minor traffic violation. The officer approaches your car, and through the window he sees a gun lying on the seat next to you. Regardless of what action he takes, what do you think will go through his mind? Now, change the gun to a hammer, and if you'd like, scatter a tape measure and a few other tools across the seat. Or change the gun to a softball bat and drop a mitt holding a ball next to it. Will these two scenarios be viewed differently by the officer than the one with the gun? Of course they will.

No, neither the hammer or bat is as good a weapon as the gun. But remember that the Okinawans would have preferred *katanas*, too. Sometimes you have to make do with what you have.

Tools also have the additional advantage of being viewed somewhat like the cane if you're brought to court for defending yourself. Stab someone who breaks into your house with a $500 custom fighting knife and you may rest assured the prosecution will try to convince the jury that only a maniac would even own such an item. Do

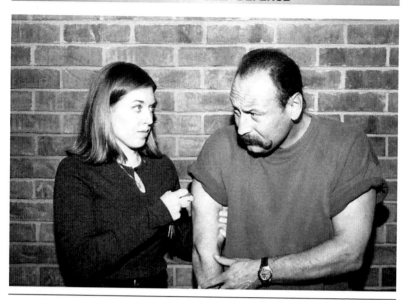

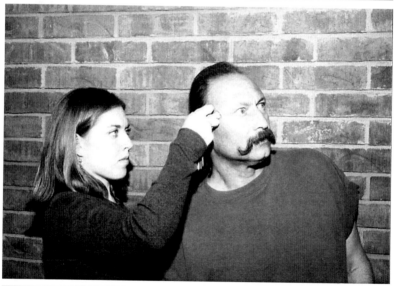

Small impact weapons, such as the COMTECH Stinger shown here, are applicable to a variety of threat levels. Applied to nerve centers or muscles, the COMTECH can repel a low-level attack. A strike to the temple or other vital area is called for if the peril is sufficient.

exactly the same thing with the knife you used last Thanksgiving to carve turkey for your grandchildren and your own attorney can bring that up himself. Now, don't get me wrong: it makes perfect sense to me to have the very best weapons technology can offer, and as long as it's not just some stupid gimmick, I upgrade every time a new defensive product comes out. But once again, we are living in a society turned upside down. Many people still believe it's okay to defend yourself in an emergency but view any preparation for such defense with suspicion. In other words, if you're cutting weeds in your backyard with a sickle, someone attacks you, and you're forced to kill him with the sickle, that's one thing. If you're in the same backyard practicing with your sword when the attack occurs, the same people who would have understood the sickle will wonder why you'd want to be doing such a thing in the first place (unless they're of the warrior mind-set).

Don't ask me to explain this kind of thinking; it's like it's okay to survive as long as you did so more by luck than by preparation. But that's pretty much where we stand in today's upside-down society. As I said, my first choice for defense would be an item specifically designed for such a task. But I can't predict the specific political or legal environment within which you may be called upon to defend your life, and sometimes a weapon that is also a tool may be a better choice. In any case, you should be aware of the different strategies legal opposition may try to apply to make your justifiable act look like murder or manslaughter. Once again, the foresight that prepares you for self-defense and enables you to stay alive physically may work against you in court. The prosecutor will do his best to make it look as if merely having a weapon ready when you needed it shows malice aforethought.

That said, my personal self-defense system includes a firearm, knife, and at least one impact weapon. Each has its role, and each is considered the "primary" weapon at certain threat levels. In turn, each acts as a backup to the others should one be lost, unreachable, or rendered useless for any other reason. If you've learned nothing else in this chapter, remember that nonlethal weapons should be only part of the overall package and are not to be used in life-threatening situations unless they are all you have. Even then, they should be employed jointly with unarmed combat techniques.

Which it's time to get into now.

There is no weapon too short for a brave man.
—Richard Steele, *The Guardian*, 1713

9

Unarmed Combat

Simple Equals Effective

Once a wise man was asked, What is intelligence? He answered, modesty. Then he was asked, What is modesty? And he answered, intelligence.

—Solomon Ben Judah Ibn Gabirol
The Improvement of Character, III, c. 1050

Once again, I feel obligated to stress that if death, rape, or serious bodily harm is to be the consequence of defeat, you're much better off using a weapon to protect yourself than going at it with your bare hands. Personally, I do my best to never be completely unarmed, anytime, anywhere—not asleep, not on commercial airlines, and not bathing. I sleep wearing one of Newt Livesay's excellent Woo neck knives, and there is always a pistol, flashlight, and larger knife hidden near the bed. On commercial airlines I stay legal, carrying folding knives well under the 4-inch blade limit and a cane. In the showers of our house I keep plastic knives or old blades I don't care about rusting. You may call me paranoid if you like. I will smile, and although I probably won't bother saying it, I will think of you as naive. I have seen a great deal of violence during my lifetime, and I know firsthand that it can occur when one least expects it. Like when you're mailing a letter at the post office in Edmond, Oklahoma. Or eating a Big Mac at a California McDonald's.

That out of the way again, there are several very good reasons to incorporate empty-hand skills into your self-defense package. Try as you might, you may, for one reason or another, be forced to be unarmed. You may be attacked too fast to draw your weapon, or you may be unable to access it for some other reason. In addition, all of the unarmed techniques we're about to look at are useful in conjunction with hand-held weapons like knives, sticks, and even firearms at close range. This is important to keep in mind as you read on: just because you've picked up a weapon doesn't mean you've lost the use of the rest of your body.

As I stated in the introduction, this is a catalog of concepts concerning self-defense, not another "how to fight" book. There are more than enough of those on the market already. More than 50 years after it was first written, *Kill or Get Killed* by Col. Rex Applegate is still the best, and I hold no misconceptions that I could improve upon its practical approach to realistic techniques for close-quarters combat. My primary concern, both in the classes I teach and within this text, is that while in today's world we have literally thousands of fighters who are well-trained physically, most have never had to actually fight for real, and because of this that final element essential to the development of the warrior mind-set is missing. Yes, no matter how much you train, or how many different training approaches you take, the "real thing" is a little different. If you've got an IQ 10 points above the average rock you know that intuitively, and that knowledge gives birth to a little voice in the back of your head that keeps saying, "I wonder if it really works." Since you can't just go out and arbitrarily pick fights to test the waters, the next best thing is to hear someone who has actually done so say, "Yeah, I did that, and yeah, it really works." So that's exactly what I plan to do.

What you're about to be introduced to if you're a beginner, or what will be a partial review if you have already studied practical self-defense, are the techniques that I personally *know* can work because I've used them. In some cases I used them in arrest situations as a police officer or in out-and-out brawls while portraying a criminal undercover. Others I used during encounters I had in my younger years when I spent lots of time in places where it is unwise to spend lots of time. Regardless of the conditions under which they were used, they worked. I am staying away from the more complex joint locks, takedowns, come-alongs, throws, and restraints for two reasons: 1) they are harder to learn and must almost always be viewed to be understood, let alone learned, and 2) I have never used any of them on an aggressive attacker without first "softening him up" with a strike or two. This is not surprising since I am a "hitter at heart," and the various methods of what the Japanese call *atemi* (striking) have always been my most natural initial response as a counter to a violent attack. There are those, however, who are not of this "mind-set within a mind-set," so please do not interpret this as a proclamation against all "grabbing techniques." Nor should this chapter be viewed as a complete inventory. There are other techniques I am 99-percent sure would be effective; I just haven't reached the 100-percent mark by using them myself.

What you are going to read about in this chapter are techniques that are very basic and easy to learn, because that's what I always found to work for me—basic and simple. There is nothing mysterious about them, so I'm afraid anyone who bought this book hoping to finally discover that elusive magic "death blow" he's always heard about is going to be sorely disappointed.

In real-life close-quarters combat, what counts are speed, accuracy, and adequate power. Flying side, spinning back, and triple-flip-with-a-half-gainer roundhouse kicks are far more dramatic than simply driving a thumb through an assailant's eye socket or kicking him in the knee, but try the fancy stuff for real and you'll get your butt beat by even the most mundane streetfighter. Keep in mind that the "perfect form" your senseis have stressed over the years is not nearly as important in a streetfight as it is in kata competition. This principle is expressed well by my friend Hock Hochheim when he says, "The only time I look pretty is when it's by accident."

Some of these techniques will come easily and feel natural to you. Others will seem more awkward. This is normal—we're all different, and some people just "take" to some things better than others do. Perfect your favorite techniques and hope that if you are attacked you will be in a position to use them. But practice the ones that feel clumsy too; you may find yourself in a situation in which your preferred strikes simply won't be practical.

To further your education, get a chart of pressure points and begin thinking about which strikes would be appropriate to the different weak spots of the human body. Another, always easier and sometimes better way is to use your own body as the chart. Start at the top of your head and begin pushing, pulling, and tapping your way down to your feet. Every time you feel pain or sense weakness in the physiological structure, you've come to a target area. Another method of advanced study is to get a copy of the rules of all the fighting sports you can find. Boxing, wrestling, judo, karate—get them all. Find out what's against the rules, then cheat. The reason they're against the rules of these sports is because they work. (Don't forget Mike Tyson's ear-biting technique.)

Okay, let's look at the things that have allowed me to live long enough to get this receding hairline and middle-aged weight problem.

The kicks that are practical for true self-defense are low—groin level and below. High kicking is fine for stretching and practice; if you learn to kick high, kicking low becomes easier. But for self-defense, high kicks are too easy to see coming and too easy to block. Of course, if your opponent is on the ground and you're still standing, his head and other higher areas become low targets. But beware: as I've already pointed out, heads are hard. I once kicked a college offensive tackle in the jaw with what I thought was a pretty good front kick wearing cowboy boots. This 300-plus pound coked-to-the-gills gorilla turned away from the guy he was choking on the ground, said, "You're next," then went back to strangling his victim. This kind of thing can make your blood curdle. I had to beat him over the head with a chair and knock him unconscious before I convinced him to stop.

Kick hard and low to the groin, shins, ankles, insteps, and especially the knees. I recommend turning the foot slightly outward and using the entire sole to the knee to create a larger margin for error. (With the toes, ball of the foot, and heel it's too easy to miss or glance off.) Knees are fragile, and it doesn't take much to send your attacker to an orthopedic surgeon if you do it right. Many of the low front and side thrust kicks found in karate and tae kwon do are good, and if you've been practicing them for years, keep using them. Some of the Filipino systems—sikaran to mention only one—also teach practical kicking. Likewise, if you've studied Thai boxing you've developed some exceptionally strong and destructive kicking techniques. But if you haven't already spent hours, weeks, or years learning the correct kicking form, don't sweat it. Practice on a heavy bag, kicking post, and other targets will help you create your own form and muscle memory. If you're hitting the target hard and not falling down in the process, you're doing it right. As elemental as it may seem, I have always found a feint to the head before kicking low to be quite effective.

The knee kick or strike is an extremely powerful blow when delivered correctly. Again, if you've practiced Muay Thai, you can not only skip over this paragraph, you could have written it yourself. A knee to the groin, the thigh muscles, or lower abdomen may end a fight in and of itself. (Notice I said may, not will. Never count on any one technique being enough.) If one knee strike doubles your opponent over, use another to strike his face. Clasping the hands behind his neck while you do this stabilizes both you and your target and adds force to the blow as you push his face down into your rising leg. If you find yourself behind your opponent and in a good position for it, a knee to the spine can also be disabling.

The hands are the most easily controlled natural weapons we have because we use them so much for everyday tasks. They are much faster than the feet, and what they give up in power (almost everyone's legs are stronger than their arms) they make up for with speed. If you've spent long years developing your fistics through one of the punching sports like karate or boxing, do not throw the baby out with the bath water. Punch. As for myself, I've gotten away from the closed fist as much as possible for two reasons: 1) I found I could deliver more power with an open hand, and 2) I'm not as likely to break my knuckles. (I've done this a few times and never really grew fond of it.)

Let me explain why more power can be delivered with the open hand. Many of you have no doubt been to some martial arts demonstration at which you witnessed the "unbendable arm" exhibition. For those of you unfamiliar with it, the demonstrator lays his outstretched arm, palm up, over the shoulder of a volunteer. He then clenches his fist, tightens his arm, and fights to keep it from bending while the volunteer (and sometimes other volunteers if the demonstrator is strong) attempt to bend his arm. Fight as the demonstrator will, strong as he may be, eventually, enough people are able to bend it.

Then the performer shakes his arm to loosen it and gives a little speech about the power of *ki* (Japanese for "inner power"; *chi* in Chinese). Now he extends his arm over the volunteer's shoulder again but leaves it relaxed with his fingers open and loose. Often letting a tranquil look fall over his face to add to the performance, he allows his assistants to pull on his arm again. The arm bends slightly, then stops and will not bend further.

Oooooooh! Ahhhhhhh! the audience breathes, not unlike spectators at a Fourth of July fireworks show. They go home just knowing that Mr. Magic Ki-Man knows all kinds of Asian secrets and could probably even sit across the room and bend spoons with mental power alone if he so chose.

I hate to burst the bubble for some of you New Age Zen-heads but the "secret" behind the unbendable arm is far less mystical and has little, if anything, to do with ki. (Ki does exist; it's just not as enigmatic and elusive as some would have you believe.) The answer is simple body mechanics. When you extend your arm, as in pushing (or striking) you use the triceps muscle. When you retract your arm, as in pulling something toward you, the biceps is used. Our bodies are constructed so that when the muscle on one side of a bone contracts in use, the muscle on the other side relaxes. Therefore, when we push away (as in striking or extending the arm over the shoulder of an unsuspecting volunteer) the triceps automatically goes to work while the biceps should loosen. When the "unbendable arm" demonstrator consciously overrides this natural tendency and purposely tightens the entire arm, his biceps and triceps work against each other, and he actually weakens himself, assisting the volunteers in bending the arm. When he leaves it loose, however, the triceps works alone, as it was designed to, and he is much stronger.

Now, when we push something away from us (again, the same movement as striking out) we are using our triceps. And we use an open hand to push. But when we pull something toward us, we grab, clenching our fingers around the object, which is similar to making a fist. All your life you have unconsciously trained your clenched fingers to act in conjunction with a contracted biceps, so when you make a fist, the biceps automatically tightens in preparation for pulling. Lots of practice can overcome this, to a degree. But after 30 years of punching (and I do continue to practice it some), I still find myself sometimes unconsciously tightening the biceps. This results in a loss of speed, and therefore power, which is enough to convince me that even after all these years of training I am still performing a movement that is forced rather than natural. Also, keep in mind that the power of a strike is generated by the speed with which the hand moves from its starting point to its target—not from how strong, or tight, the muscles that deliver the blow happen to be. (You scientific-minded people, go back to that Geology 1113 class you took as freshmen and remember how a river's force comes from speed, not size.) You're welcome to agree or disagree (I mean, I have been telling you to think on your own all through this book, haven't I?), but this should be food for thought, even among dissenters.

Most "punching" techniques can also be done with what is called the palm-heel strike. I had a little problem with three guys who wanted my money in Copenhagen, Denmark, one time, and a heel-palm strike up under the nose to one of them got his mind off my money and onto his own problems. Self-defense is like anything else: if something works for you once, you tend to rely on it again. So the second guy got the equivalent of a left hook to the side of the head—but with an open hand. The third guy was so drunk he could barely stand up, and all three decided to go look for easier prey.

Jabs, hooks, crosses, karate lunge and reverse punches—all can be employed by opening the hand and curling the fingers back, then striking with the heel of the palm. The only downsides are that you lose about one inch of reach and that your palm has more padding and therefore a little more "give" to it than your bony knuckles. Both, I believe, are more than compensated for by the extra energy generated, and the fact that if you hit something harder than your knuckles you won't go hopping away holding them in your other hand like the buffoon in some bad TV sitcom.

An excellent technique that I used once in my early 20s is the double-slap to the ears, sometimes called the ear-concussion blow. If you cup your hands you can rupture the attacker's eardrums and actually cause unconsciousness. I didn't do that, since this was not really a life-threatening situation. But I did feel it was necessary to impress upon the man that both my girlfriend and I would appreciate it if he'd quit pinching her breasts. I kept my fingers open rather than cupping them, and it still turned his equilibrium into a jar of Welch's grape jelly. At least I had to hold him up by his hair and beard while I explained why his behavior was inappropriate.

The sides of the hand (both front and back—*shuto* and *haito* to you karate buffs), or chops, are also excellent striking areas. The force of these blows is distributed along a line, however, so they work better on some areas of the opponent's body than others. The neck, throat, collarbone, and other areas that the side of the hand "fits into" are perfect. A strike to an area such as the chest, however, takes tremendous force to stop even a reasonably strong attacker. During a really nasty arrest situation one time, one in which I'd have used a baton if I'd had one with me, I caught a guy on the collarbone with a chop like this. We had to take him to the hospital before booking him into jail. Again, refer to the chart (or your own body) for target areas, and use a little common sense.

Finger strikes are excellent to the eyes. Eyes are more than a painful and debilitating target; they're a great psychological mark as well. Like most men, I have two areas of my body that I'm scared to death of losing. They both come in pairs, and the eyes are one of them. Forego the Three Stooges "pick two, nyuk nyuk" approach and open the entire hand. Aim for the eyes with the middle and ring finger, and you create a margin for error in case your aim is slightly off. You'll have the index finger on one side, and the little finger on the other, and unless you've really misjudged your target, something ought to find its way into at least one of the "windows to your attacker's soul." If it's a really serious threat you're facing, as long as your fingers are already there in the sockets, you might as well dig around a little before extracting them. Unlike the other specific techniques I'm recommending, I've never actually poked anyone in the eyes. But I know it works because I've been poked. Had I been alone, I'd have been in big trouble. Luckily, my partner handled the rest of the situation while I backed away and tried not to cry. And ladies, some of you have beautiful little daggers growing from your fingers that can carry eye attacks into a whole new dimension.

Gouging into the eyes with the thumbs is another good tactic, but it's easier in close-in or "grappling" situations. Striking out at arm's length with the thumbs is a little clumsier and gives no margin for error like striking with the fingers. But if you are close enough and in a position to first grab the attacker's face or the sides of his head to ground the target, you can then work your thumbs into the sockets. Sound gross? It is. Getting raped or murdered is even grosser.

The palm, the side of the hand, or even the open fingers themselves coming up into the testicles can stop or at least startle the toughest of men. Again, as with the eyes, men have got a real fear factor going in this area—we don't want to lose those babies. As a cop, when I'd be facing someone who suddenly knew he was about to be arrested, and I could see on his face that he wasn't going to submit easily, I often flipped my open fingers up into his groin. This almost always stunned him long enough to get around back and put the bracelets on. It's fast and also low key, and therefore hard to spot by witnesses who simply don't understand that you're not starting a fight; you're stopping one before it gets started. Again, as with the eyes, if it's a more serious situation, and as long as you've got your hand down there, you can grab hold and start squeezing and twisting. I know—I don't like the idea of touching some maggot's privates any more than you do, even through his pants. But I like the idea of him touching mine, or killing me, even less. The open fingers can be used in this same manner to any soft or extremely sensitive part of the body.

Lips and ears can be torn off, but in reality they don't come off nearly as easy as you might think. I tried an ear one time and didn't get it done. But I've also had it tried on me, and I can vouch for the fact that it sure does hurt, and it might be just the thing for that unruly brother-in-law.

Other viable open-hand techniques include reaching into the throat and crushing the windpipe and twisting and breaking fingers or other small joints. As I said earlier on, I'm not going to get into complex joint manipulation, but suffice it to say that there's a golden rule you can go by in this area: all joints of the human body were designed to bend certain ways and not others. Bend or twist them in ways they weren't meant to go or hyperextend them in the ways they were, and severe pain, broken bones, and torn ligaments and cartilages will be the result.

Because of the build God gave me (which will never get me an invitation to the Mr. Olympia contest but does include some fairly powerful shoulders), I have always favored overhand blows. With one overhead hammer hand (closed fist but using the bottom of the hand rather than the knuckles), the palm-heel strike, or the chop, I have been able to stop a lot of problems before they got too far out of hand. Conversely, with a straight punch I have never seemed to generate the energy of which I felt I should be capable. Your strong and weak techniques may not be the same as mine, but this is why it is vitally important that you get out in the garage and start experimenting with the heavy bag or something that can give you some feedback as to how hard you're hitting. If you feel something just isn't working for you, give it some time and keep practicing and trying it in new ways. (As they say, maybe you're just holding your mouth wrong.) But if you finally reach the point where you've exhausted every possibility of taking that technique to the fullest, accept the fact that this specific move isn't going to be your strong suit. You should still practice it and keep it in your unarmed arsenal, because you may find yourself in a predicament in which it is the only feasible thing to do. In such cases, it should be considered a "softening technique" which can set up your better defenses.

Head butts are very good if done properly. Right about at the hairline (a little below my hairline these days), your skull is extremely hard. Driving it into an opponent's nose, or any other fragile area, can be devastating, but remember that there is a very small margin for error here. Misjudge your target, even a little, and it may be you lying on the sidewalk and listening to the little birdies chirp. I've done this only once, and I did it "kind of right and kind of wrong." I didn't knock myself out, but it sure hurt during the rest of the encounter.

Your teeth are another weapon God gave you with which to defend yourself. During a football game years ago, against a team that was living up to its reputation for dirty play, I got my helmet knocked off making a tackle and then found myself at the bottom of a pile. Right in front of my eyes, amidst the tangle of arms and legs, I could see a calf just below a kneepad of the opposing team's color. I'd been spit on, kicked in the groin, and subjected to every other breach of the rules you can imagine during that game. I recall thinking, "The Lord works in mysterious ways," as I bit down. The howling was just terrible.

I'm a big believer in elbow strikes—up, down, forward and backward—because they've always worked great for me both standing and on the ground. I suspect I find them effective because of a combination of natural shoulder power and the fact that I practiced a football technique called the forearm shiver for many years of my life. The forearm shiver is quite similar to an upward or rising elbow strike—you just make contact with the forearm instead of the elbow—and it can be an effective power technique on its own. Over the years I've found it works even better when your opponent isn't wearing a helmet and face mask. (Glad I didn't get one myself during "the bite.")

One of the fastest techniques is the back fist. It should be employed with a "whipping" motion that snaps into the target, not tightening until the last split second before contact. Many people think of the back fist as nothing more than a stunning technique, but when executed well, it is powerful in and of itself. The only time over the last 30 years I've accidentally hit one of my students was with a back fist. We were sparring, and he stepped in just as I threw it. The timing could not have been worse—for either of us. I knocked out two of his teeth, and he fell about 5 feet backward onto his back. His teeth sliced open my knuckles and we went to the hospital together. As you might guess, I felt terrible that I'd hurt him. But we both

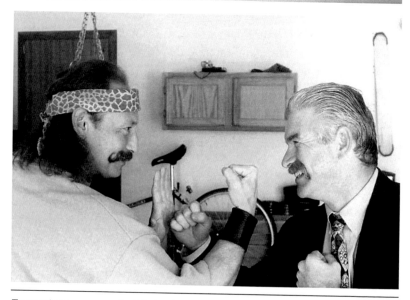

Twenty-five years ago, bad timing in the dojo cost this man a couple teeth and me some stitches. But it proved to both of us that the backfist had been underrated. He's an attorney now (even looks like one, doesn't he?), and he still hasn't sued me.

learned that the back fist works. (Twenty-five years later, we're still friends. In fact, he's a lawyer now, and he still hasn't sued me.)

No, I haven't covered all the techniques that will work in practical unarmed self-defense. Covering everything in one volume is impossible. Besides that, you aren't even going to get a glimpse of what might work for you personally until you actually put this book down and start practicing. But that's what the next chapter is all about. So let's move on.

The superior man is distressed by the limitations of his ability; he is not distressed by the fact that men do not recognize the ability that he has.

—Confucius
Analects, XV, c. 500 B.C.

TRAINING

10

Training and the Psychological Motivation to Train

Oft bend the bow, and thoust with ease shalt do,
What others with can't all their strength put to.
— Robert Herrick
Hesperides, 1648

Self-defense is no different from every other aspect of life: there is a tremendous difference between acquiring an academic knowledge of the subject and possessing the ability to put that knowledge into practice.

I hope you learn something from this book. And there are other good books, manuals, and videos that can be extremely helpful in your quest to grasp the concepts of personal protection. But reading and watching can do no more than give you an intellectual understanding of self-defense; actually being able to perform the techniques is quite another matter. Effective self-defense requires enough repetitive practice to develop what we often call "reflexive action" or "muscle memory." It has to come so naturally that you do it without having to think about it. And self-defense requires an even more deep-seeded muscle memory than most things because your actions must be performed under tremendous stress—a psychological state in which all but the most deeply ingrained learning scatters from the mind like feathers in a tornado.

My first glimpse of the difference between academic knowledge and tangible execution came to me in junior high. George Davis lived right across the street from me and had been one of my best friends for years. But, as is the case with most normal young men, there was also a lot of competition between us. You see, George and I were the biggest kids in our class, and the question of which one of us could "beat up" the other (pretty important stuff in those days) had always loomed over our heads. Through tacit agreement, we had avoided finding out the answer. Then, a physical education class section on wrestling came along, and finding out who was "tougher" (at least within the controlled atmosphere of a closely refereed wrestling match) made finding out unavoidable.

George and I were both in the heavyweight class. But we had come up through different brackets in the tournament, and one night I found myself sitting at home in my room, scheduled to wrestle George the next morning for the seventh grade championship. Through my window, I could see the light on in George's room across the street. (This is also a good example of what we talked about in Chapter 2—situations in which you have too much time to think and let your imagination run wild.) To put it bluntly, I was scared. I wasn't afraid of getting hurt—that wasn't going to happen in a junior high wrestling match. What terrified me was the humiliation of defeat.

As adults, we sometimes forget that children's problems and fears are just as real to them as ours are to us. Although during the early 1960s terms like "self image" were not in a 12-year-old's vocabulary, I can look back on it now and see that much of the way I viewed myself at the time was tied up in being big, strong, and tough. If I lost to George the next morning, who would I be? Would the sun even rise in the sky the next day?

Then I got an idea.

I was always one of those kids who sent away for self-defense and martial arts books advertised in Superman and Marvel comics.

Junior Judo, American Combat Judo, Ketsugo—I had 'em all. So I pulled out my books and started studying. By bedtime my confidence had returned because now I had a plan: I would beat George using the secret "Japanese tricks" I knew and he didn't, and I didn't figure anyone in 1963 Enid, Oklahoma, was likely to recognize that I was cheating.

The next morning George and I stepped out onto the mat. The gym coach blew the whistle, and the match began. Ten seconds later I was pinned on my back and the whistle was blowing again.

Although I had to suffer through a little ribbing in the cafeteria that day at lunch, no one but me seemed to even remember the match the next day. The sun *did* keep coming up every morning, and life pretty much went on the way it had. Thirty-five years later, the details of the match are only one of those vague, hazy memories of childhood to me, and if George remembers it at all I'd be surprised. What I have retained since then, however, is the understanding that there's a big difference between reading about how to do something and being able to do it.

If you intend to become effective at self-defense, you will have to practice. But practicing anything often takes more than simple self-discipline; sometimes we must play little psychological games with ourselves to become, and remain, motivated. As human beings we tend to practice the things we like, neglect the things we don't like, and our motivations sometimes have little, if anything, to do with how important those things are. Through a complex series of rationalization, we convince ourselves that what we like is important and what we don't like is not. Perhaps another personal anecdote can better explain this.

As I've already hinted at earlier, my father had a completely different personality than I did, with completely different priorities, likes, and dislikes. Even though Dad was a very talented athlete (he played one season for the Philadelphia Eagles), I don't think he ever really enjoyed it. When his football career ended, he abruptly halted all physical exercise. What he liked was business and civic work. So he practiced business and civic work, and he excelled at both.

Business has always bored me to tears, and although I loved my father like—well, like a father, I guess—the period of time I spent working for him was literally the most miserable of my life. (I hold no illusions that it was any fun for him, either.) His attempts to interest me in tasks such as putting little bitty numbers into little bitty boxes on ledger sheets came close to killing us both. (Luckily, my mother was usually around to keep things from coming to blows.)

As soon as the "five o'clock whistle" blew, if I hadn't already found some excuse to get out of the office, I was off to the dojo or gym to practice martial arts or lift weights. I wanted to do something *I liked*. Dad, of course, stayed late at the office practicing more of what *he liked*—business. The bottom line? We both thought the other was lazy.

Are exercise and the ability to defend yourself important? Yes. Is being able to balance accounts on a ledger sheet important? Yes. Was my father incapable of exercising? No. Was I too stupid to balance the accounts? No. It's just that neither of us wanted to do things we didn't like to do, and I don't think we were much different from 99 percent of the rest of the world in that respect.

Some of you reading this are like me, and some of you are more like my father. Those of you like me are going to take to self-defense practice like the ducks in my backyard take to the pond. But, even if you recognize the importance of self-defense, you "Dads" out there are going to have a harder time getting yourselves to practice. I will grudgingly concede that someone has to keep the books if a business is to be successful, but it was like pulling teeth to get myself to do it. In that same sense, it's going to take extra effort for some of you to force yourselves to go to the gym or out into the backyard or garage and start hitting the heavy bag.

Here's a little visual imagery that might help inspire you. Picture yourself still sitting in that reclining chair. You've just finished reading this book and are thinking, "Yeah, now I know what to do if I need to," but you have not yet actually practiced any of the techniques. Now picture George Davis (we're still close friends, and he's no longer 12 years old; in fact, he's about six feet six and 250 pounds) bursting through your front door and slamming your butt all over the living room. Because that's exactly what's going to happen if you get attacked and haven't made the bridge between academic knowledge and muscle memory. Keep in mind, however, that your "George" isn't going to be a 12-year-old boy or the fine grown man George has become since then. Your "George" is going to be the biggest, baddest rapist or murderer you've ever dreamed of meeting in your worst nightmare.

What inspires you to train is a personal thing, and you'll have to come up with your own individual motivations. But if you recognize the need and are not like those of us who like it, you might also think of training similarly to the way I view computers: computers are like business to me. I don't like them (actually, I think of them as television's "evil twin"); I don't understand them, I don't trust them, and I have no interest in them. But I've had to learn how to use a computer, at least at its most rudimentary levels, in order to write. Believe me, I am no black belt in computerology and barely know a dot-com from an e-mail. But I forced myself to learn enough to get by. You don't have to become the self-defense equivalent of a computer geek to defend yourself, either. All you have to be able to do is master the basics.

So how are you going to practice? One way is with a good instructor, and we'll talk about how to pick a good one—and how to avoid the bad ones—in the next chapter. If you are close enough to some of the people I recommend or find another teacher who fits the bill, by all means lay out the cash and sign up. (Yes, I even made myself enroll in a vo-tech school computer course a few years ago.) But a lot of you are going to find that time, money, geography, or other problems make it difficult for you to take this path. So remember what Musashi said: you *can* teach yourself.

For the rest of this chapter we'll assume that home study is the route you're going to take. The easiest way to get you started is probably to just explain what I do myself when I train at home. First, there are a few pieces of equipment in which I would strongly suggest you invest. In my own garage I have a heavy bag, a double-ended striking ball, a speed bag, a cutting dummy, a cutting/striking post, focus mitts, an arm shield pad, weights, and a couple of lifting benches. Boxing gloves come in handy, and you can invest as much or as little in other protective gear as you think you need. Keep in mind that you may already have some useful items around the house. Did your son play catcher on the Little League team? Then you've probably still got some serviceable shin guards, a mask, and a chest protector rotting away up in the attic. Full-contact practice sticks of varying lengths are easy to make with PVC pipe covered in foam rubber. If you're going to carry a cane for self-defense, make training canes for you and your partner. (You can use the real thing on the bags.) You're only limited by your imagination. Now let's look at what you can learn and practice with these things.

The heavy bag provides the feel of actual contact for kicks, punches, and other strikes. (Years ago, an out-of-town brown belt dropped in to train in my dojo. He demonstrated beautiful kicks in the air but had never kicked anything but air and fell down when I had him kick the bag.) Striking something is very different from striking nothing. It takes different balance, timing, and recovery.

Extended heavy bag workouts are also great for endurance. While the average self-defense encounter is over long before endurance plays a very big part, there's no guarantee that your confrontation is going to be one of the average ones. The heavy bag (and indeed most of your self-defense training program) can be worked into a daily physical fitness routine, which will "kill two birds with one stone." The heavy bag is also valuable when practicing with canes, other sticks, and rubber, wooden, or blunt aluminum training knives. Need I mention what will happen if you use a real knife against the bag, especially a water-filled one like mine?

The double-end striking ball teaches speed, blocking, dodging, and footwork. It's great for working out hand, elbow, and even head strike combinations, and when set low enough to the ground it can be a good trainer for kicking. Make sure the elastic cords are tight enough to provide a fast enough return to be a challenge. That way you'll have the added benefit of learning to duck, bob, and weave, or else you'll get really good at taking shots to the face. Probably a little of both. Like the heavy bag, the double-end ball can also be used in conjunction with sticks and training knives.

The boxer's speed bag is for timing and coordination. Almost all large sporting good stores carry speed bag packages that contain the

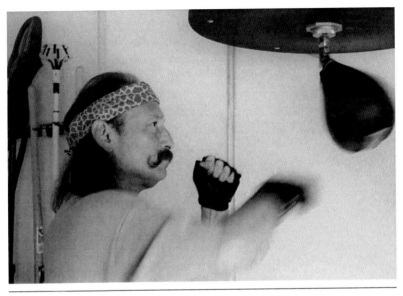

Equipment such as the boxer's speed bag can build timing, reflexes, and endurance when training alone.

bag, frame, and bolts and screws to mount it to your wall. The bags in these combo packs are usually about the right size for beginners. As you progress, you will want to substitute smaller and faster speed bags, gradually working down to the "peanut" bags used by pros. To start off, just follow the instructions in the box. After you've mastered that, a little creativity will find you working out new routines on your own. At first, the short striking movements necessary to keeping the rhythm going may not appear to have any real relationship to actual combat strikes. Don't let that bother you. Over time, the hand speed and coordination you develop will be transposed into your other training. I mean, let's face it, if these things didn't have some value, would every boxing gym in the world be equipped with them?

I used to use bag gloves when I worked the bags, then it suddenly struck me that I don't wear bag gloves when I walk down the street and am not very likely to have them on if I get attacked. Now I either practice with bare hands or wear thin leather weight-lifting gloves (with open fingers) to keep from skinning my knuckles. During my old days of karate, I used to pound a *makiwara* board until my knuckles swelled up and bled, drive my fist into tubs of rice to build calluses, and do all kinds of other ridiculous things. Following the same logic I did when I quit wearing bag gloves, I suddenly realized I was not living in ancient Okinawa, and that the threat of the Japanese coming over the hill to attack me every day was not likely, so I decided that it might be wiser to practice in ways that would not lead to arthritis and other orthopedic problems later in life. Later life is now here, and on cold rainy days I now wish I'd decided that earlier. You young studs might want to take note of that before you find yourself saying the same thing.

Since I don't walk around town with my wrists wrapped, I rarely do that anymore either. I prefer to strengthen the wrist itself. The only time I stray from that rule is if I intend to work the heavy bag round after round for conditioning—to the point where I know my joints will be too sore to type the next day if I don't wrap them.

Few of us wear a judo, karate, arnis, or kung fu uniform in everyday life, either. Therefore, it makes little sense to train for realistic combat in them. There's a tremendous difference in freedom of movement when wearing street clothes versus a gi, and the odds are overwhelmingly in favor of your needing to defend yourself when wearing everyday clothing. You can get by training in a gi, sweat suit, or gym shorts some of the time, but you should conduct a large part of your practice dressed as you normally would be. If you wear a business suit five days out of the week, find an old sport coat, tie, and pair of slacks to train in. If you do construction work and have steel-toed boots on your feet day in and day out, practice in them. You'll find that kicking in boots is far different from kicking barefoot or in martial arts shoes or cross-trainers. It's slower, and just like kicking a heavy bag instead of kicking in the air, your balance and recovery must be adjusted accordingly. (But those steel toes do have their advantages!) The bottom line here is that you should train in the type of clothing that you are most likely to be wearing if attacked. The more normal you feel, the more automatic your responses will be, and the chances of your survival will increase dramatically.

My cutting dummy's name is Rip. Rip's made of an old pair of

At least some of your training should take place in the type of clothes you wear on an everyday basis. Moving in slacks and a sport coat is different than in a gi or sweat suit. Likewise, kicking in boots or dress shoes requires different timing than when barefoot or wearing athletic shoes.

jeans and a heavy shirt packed with wet newspapers and the scraps of old jeans and shirts that used to be his "skin." This allows practice with live blades and gives me an idea of which ones cut and penetrate better than others. Sometimes I'm surprised. Without naming any brand names, let me say that I've found several low-end knives to work quite well and a few high-priced blades, touted as "the best," to be all but worthless. This is good stuff to know ahead of time if you ever face a life-and-death encounter. (Think of how embarrassing it would be to be found dead with a $1,000 custom "battle blade" in your hand that wouldn't cut.) Rip is also useful for focus work with sticks and unarmed techniques.

The cutting/striking post is just what the name implies—a wooden post. It serves a little different function than Rip in that, like the heavy bag, it provides heavy resistance to strikes with both knives and sticks. Again, hitting something hard (like human bone) gives a different feel than hitting something soft or just swishing your weapon through the air. More than one man who considered himself competently trained has found his knife or stick flying from his hand at an inopportune time.

So far, everything we've discussed revolves around training that you can do by yourself. The focus mitts and similar equipment require a partner. The focus mitts look vaguely like a catcher's mitt (and if you found one up in the attic next to your son's old chest protector you might as well try it before shelling out the cash for the real thing) and are worn by one person while the other strikes. The man wearing the mitts can hold them at different levels and angles as well as moving them around like real human opponents. The arm shield pads are used in similar fashion and are often better for kicking practice. I find both these training items to be extremely valuable.

Bags and other training equipment move when you hit them—but they don't move the same way humans do. And bags don't react at all until they're actually struck. Humans have a nasty habit of trying to get out of the line of fire as soon as they perceive a threat. Prearranged drills can be helpful for timing, but their very name tells you that they will not prepare you for unrehearsed attack. For this reason, some actual free fighting or sparring with your training partner is valuable if (and this is a very big IF) it is kept in perspective.

Sparring, no matter how hard you go at it, is not real self-defense. You are wearing protective gear you would not have on in a real situation, or you are "pulling your punches." Unless you are insane, you are using nonlethal trainers when you spar with weapons. This creates an atmosphere in which both you and your partner know that you are not facing a true life-and-death situation. When you take a slice across the wrist with a rubber training knife, the "wound" produces a "Ha ha, you got me that time" reaction rather than a severed artery. This ambience lends itself to both parties experimenting with techniques that they would not likely try in real combat. That's good; experimentation under these conditions is a great learning tool. But this half-real, half-false mind-set, be it with or without weapons, is close enough to actual combat that it can trick the beginning, intermediate, and even advanced student into believing that it is just like the real thing. Sparring is just far enough removed from reality that a false confidence can set in without your being aware of it, and this false confidence can get you killed when the real thing comes along. When I was fighting competitively in karate tournaments, I sometimes lost matches to opponents whom I have no doubt I could have beaten on the street. Likewise, I beat a few guys I would not care to meet in a dark alley.

A group of training partners is better than just one. This prepares you for opponents of different sizes, strengths, speeds, and intensities. With a training group, you can also set up multiple attacker scenarios, and you're as likely to face a situation like that today as you are a one-on-one encounter.

I didn't mention this in the chapter on firearms because it takes more than one person, so here's a good place to throw it in. Before the days of Simmunition (simulated ammunition not too different from paintballs), my SWAT team used to train with pellet guns. We wore goggles and ear protectors, and we staged little "wars" to see who could kill whom. Did the pellets hurt when they hit? You bet they did, and because they did they kept us honest. You see, this is nothing more than free fighting or sparring with guns, and the closer to reality you can get the better. The pain involved in getting hit by a .177-caliber pellet made us more wary of taking stupid chances—maybe not quite as wary as .357 Magnums would, but it definitely got us out of that "Ha ha, got me" mind-set. When you know from past experience that getting shot is going to hurt like a hornet's sting for several days, and the guys you're training with are evil-hearted demons doing their best to hit you in the crotch and other tender areas (as you're doing yourself), then your strategies get closer to reality. I'm not suggesting you do this. Sure as I do, some idiot out there is going to forget to wear his goggles, get an eye put out (just like his mother warned him he would), blame me instead of his own stupidity, and sue me. So I'm just telling you what we used to do, and that we found it to be an extremely effective method of training.

As in all training, you should begin slowly and let speed come on its own. Eventually, though, you must reach a point where all techniques are executed with as much speed as you can generate.

Sprinters will tell you that the most important aspect of their runs is the start, or how quickly they "come out of the blocks." I'm not a sprinter and never have been. So I relate this philosophy to a term I learned in football: explode. If I had a nickel for every time I've heard a football coach scream, "Explode off that line!" I could retire right now and not even have to finish this chapter. Once self-defense techniques are ingrained in your muscle memory, begin making them explode.

The regularity of your training, both with and without weapons, is far more important than the length of each session. In his book *Get Tough*, W.E. Fairbairn recommended short daily sessions, and this is advice with which I whole-heartedly agree. Don't burn yourself out, or you'll quit. A good place to start might be 10 to 15 minutes a day or 30 minutes three times a week. I've already told you how I set up paper plates in the backyard to practice shooting with my pellet revolvers. I shoot one CO_2 bottle's worth every evening, which gets me about 80 to 100 shots. Then I stop, even when I'm having fun and feel like shooting more. That way, I'm looking forward to it the next night.

When you must motivate yourself (rather than having a coach who constantly threatens you with wind sprints, push-ups, or other tortures), you should always stop training still wanting to train a little more. If you incorporate self-defense training into a fitness program like I've already suggested, it can be fun and you'll probably find yourself gradually extending your workouts without thinking about it. If you don't even have fun practicing a few minutes a day, then you've got the same problem I have each month when it comes time to try to balance the checkbook, and you're just going to have to go through life worrying about "George Davis" pinning you to the mat.

I just called George, by the way, and I was wrong. Unfortunately, he does remember our seventh-grade wrestling match.

Exercitatio optimus est magister. (Practice is the best master.)
—a Latin proverb

11

Martial Arts Schools and Self-Defense Courses

The Good, the Bad, and the Dangerously Stupid

The secret to teaching is to appear to have known all your life what you learned this afternoon.
—Author unidentified

America in the late 20th and early 21st century has some real sokes, sifus, senseis, shihans, and guros, but we are also infested with charlatans wearing belts they didn't earn and calling themselves by all manner of self-conferred titles. (I've been trying to think up a good one for myself—how does His Highness VanCook sound? Until I decide, we'll just stick with Jerry.)

In addition to the outright phony instructors, there are the well-meaning but misled. These are usually teachers who have never experienced any real self-defense situations, were taught by teachers who never fought outside a tournament ring, and are presenting misguided theory that looks good on paper but won't work in reality. Each generation of these "noncombatant" black belts produces a new generation of unrealistic teachers, and the curriculum of each generation gets a little further from pragmatic street defense.

But like I said, there are good self-defense teachers out there, too.

Now, I learned a long time ago not to stick my neck out for anyone I didn't fully know and trust—not just when recommending self-defense instructors, but in any area of life. Therefore, any teacher or program on the list that follows has met at least one of the following four criteria (most have met more than one, and some have met all four): 1) I have trained with or under the chief instructor and know his program to be top-notch; 2) I know other instructors whose opinions I value who speak highly of him; 3) I have trained at least one of his students myself, and they have demonstrated valuable skills that they attribute to his program; 4) I have spoken to the chief instructor extensively enough that I believe had he been teaching "bullshito-ryu" (which is the art in which some teachers really do deserve the rank of grandmaster), I would have known it.

In most of the programs that follow, training is done in street clothes rather than a gi, since the instructors have broken away from the traditional systems and concentrate on practical self-defense. I have included a few who have not—but in these cases they all fall into category one above: I know them, and their programs, personally and can vouch for the fact that they teach in a way applicable to today's society.

This list is by no means all-inclusive; I do not know every instructor in the United States, and just because certain ones aren't mentioned does not mean they don't take an approach to teaching that is practical. But you can be sure that the following organizations, listed alphabetically, will.

These schools are scattered all over, and many of the instructors travel to give seminars. My advice is this: if you learn that any of them is giving a seminar near you, go to it. If you live within reasonable driving distance of any of the permanently based schools, enroll. But if distance is a problem, pick out the one nearest you and contact the instructor(s). There is a lot of networking between the nontraditional teachers these days, and chances are good the instructor you call will know a qualified teacher closer to you. Many of these programs also offer extremely good videotapes and/or books.

RECOMMENDED PROGRAMS

American Bando Association (ABA)/Chief Instructor: Maung Gyi, P.O. Box 2763, Atlanta, GA 30301. Dr. Gyi is a former Gurkha, and the ABA teaches the art of the Gurkha's kukri (a big knife or short sword, depending on your point of view, I guess). Most, if not all, techniques will transfer to other edged and impact weapons.

American Combatives, Inc./Chief Instructor: John Kary, 5 Heritage Park, Huntington, WV 25704 (Web site: http://www.americancombatives.com). American Combatives is one of the most pragmatic systems of no-nonsense self-defense to be found anywhere. Unarmed close-quarters combat, stick and knife, and point shooting.

American Edgewise Society/Chief Instructor: John Saucier, 1708 S. Missouri, Crossett, AR 71635. John teaches a mixed bag of Eastern and Western blade technique, as well as stick and empty-hand defense. Sponsor and instructor at the yearly Southern Steel seminar in Little Rock, Arkansas.

American Goju-Ryu/Chief Instructor: William H. Mays, 1920 W. Lindner Ave. #245, Mesa, AZ 85202. Bill was my first instructor, and he teaches in a practical way, understanding the difference between the sport, art, and defensive aspects of martial arts. A few years ago, I made a list of the five men who had most positively influenced my life. He was on it. Need I say more?

Bei-Koku Aibujutsu Ryu Hombu/Chief Instructor: Michael J. Heenan, Kansai Gaidai University, Center for International Education, 16-1 Kitakatahoko-cho, Hirakata City, Osaka 573, Japan. This formerly traditionally based system of jujitsu has modernized, incorporating divisions that include today's folding knives, firearms, and other contemporary weapons.

CODA (Combined Oriental/Defendu Arts) and STAB (Strategies and Tactics Against Blades)/Chief Instructor: Peter Robins, 17 Audley Road, Great Leighs, Chelmsford, Essex CM3 1RS, Great Britain. Defendu was Captain W.E. Fairbairn's pragmatic version of close-quarters combat, and Pete carries on this tradition with both programs.

Cold Steel, Inc./Chief Instructor: Lynn Thompson, 2128-D Knoll Drive, Ventura, CA 93003 (Web site: www.coldsteel.com). Lynn does more than just make excellent weapons. He teaches knife, stick, and other seminars on how to use them. By 1999 Cold Steel plans to have a complete training division up and running.

Combat Technologies (COMTECH)/Chief Instructor: James A. Keating, 2728 Couse Creek Road, Milton-Freewater, OR 97862 . COMTECH is also the publisher of *Modern Knives* on-line magazine (Web site: http://www.combattech.com/ E-mail: comtech@ bmi.net) and sponsor of the annual Riddle of Steel knife training seminars on the Snake River. The Riddles have become classic training adventures, and many of us return year after year. I have very close ties to this program, and they don't come any better.

Common Sense Self-Defense/Street Combat/ Chief Instructor: Bram Frank, 20505 U.S. 19 North, Number 12-256, Clearwater, FL 33764. E-mail: arnisman@aol.com. I'm honored to serve on Bram's board of advisors, and he's an excellent instructor with a wide variety of experience.

C-2 Defense Systems/Instructors: Gary Campbell and Jerry VanCook, P.O. Box 16302, Yukon, OK 73113. Yep, that's me, and by now you should have a pretty good idea of what I teach. Just read the book again if you've forgotten. Seminars and private classes only. (Campbell also teaches the Modern Method of pistol shooting, but I've forgiven him for it.)

Denton Area Knife Fighters/Chief Instructor: Charlie Porter, 206 Solar Way, Denton, TX 76207. Charlie runs an excellent program that incorporates the best of his many years of experience. He's also designed one of my favorite fighting knives—check into the "Friend" from Black Cloud Knives.

Gung Ho Chuan Association, Inc./Chief Instructor: Bob Kasper, P.O. Box 1336, Brick, NJ 08723 (E-mail: ghca@earthlink.com, Web site: http://home.earthlink.net/~ghca). I've never met Bob personally but have talked to him on the phone and read many of his articles, and he's respected by too many people whose opinions I hold in high regard not to list here. Gung Ho encompasses several other training organizations, including Kni-Com (knife combatives). It was begun by U.S. Marine trainers but is now open to all serious students.

Hocking College/Firearms Instructor: Steve Barron, Hocking College, Department of Public Safety (Police Science), 3301 Hocking Parkway, Nelsonville, OH 45764. Steve has one of the most impressive firearms resumes you could imagine and is known far and wide as an exceptional instructor. There's no better place to learn point shooting with a pistol, and by the time this comes out they plan to have added a similar program for long guns. Hocking College is associated with American Combatives, which encompasses the full range of defense as outlined in Colonel Applegate's *Kill or Get Killed*.

International Combat Hapkido Federation (ICHF)/Chief Instructor: John Pelligrini, 1859 N. Pine Isand Road, Suite 1181, Plantation, FL 33322. ICHF has divisions for unarmed combat, cane, and umbrella, and recently teamed up with Hock Hochheim, who will be teaching knife defense.

Michael Janich, P.O. Box 1307, Boulder, CO 80306. Mike has a long history of martial arts, special ops military service, and some other government work about which we don't speak. But there's nothing "spooky" about his program. Let's just say he knows firsthand what works and what doesn't.

Jiyushinkan AikiBudo/Chief Instructor: Chuck Clark, 415 S. McClintock Rd. #7, Tempe, AZ 85281 (Web site: http://www.jiyushinkai.org). I studied under Chuck and now serve on his council of advisors. He's an old Recon Marine Vietnam vet with a background in intelligence and security work who has put his skills into practice many times. Smart man. Smart program. Jiyunshinkai has several schools around the country, and they teach aikido in a way that the student can comprehend—none of that "hocus pocus, here are some weird looking moves, now figure them out for yourself" stuff.

Martinez Academy of Arms/Chief Instructor: Ramon Martinez, Studio KHDT, 330 Broome St., New York, NY 10002 (Web site: http://www.martinez-destreza.com). Maestro Martinez teaches the sword the way it was meant to be taught—as a weapon of defense, not as a sport.

Options for Personal Security/Chief Instructor: Andy Stanford, P.O. Box 489, Sebring, FL 33871. Andy is the winner of the National Tactical Invitational and offers seminars in gun, knife, and unarmed close-quarters combat in a program called Self-Protection Education Comprehensive (SPEC). His other specialties are rifle/carbine, low-light combat, surgical speed shooting, and *mind-set.* (Have you heard that term anywhere?)

PPCT Management Systems, Inc./Executive Director: Bruce K. Siddle, 500 South Illinois, Suite 3, Millstadt, IL 62260. PPCT is the largest research-based use-of-force training organization in the world, and contracts to police, government special warfare, criminal justice academies, and colleges in the United States, Canada, the United Kingdom, Hong Kong, and Australia. To date, they have trained over 40,000 such agency instructors. Now, for the good news: they'll train you, too, as a qualified civilian. One of the very best places to learn point shooting, other practical defense methods, and particularly the warrior mind-set.

Penn State Martial Arts Group/Chief Instructor: Mike Kaye, 1346 Greenwood Circle, State College, PA 16803. This is the same guy who spotted me with the cane going through airport security, so he's observant as well as proficient in self-defense. One of my favorite training partners at Riddle of Steel.

Taylor, Bob, and Associates/Chief Instructor: Bob Taylor, P.O. Box 818, Sagle, ID 83860. Known foremost for his "Hobbit" fixed blade and now the "Pocket Hobbit" folding knife, Bob teaches an aggressive system of knife defense to go with these and all of his Round Eye Knife & Tool products. Firearms, stick, and other combatives round out a modern street program.

RMCAT (Rocky Mountain Combat Application Training)/Chief Instructor: Peyton Quinn, P.O. Box 535, Lake Oswego, CO 80827 (Web site: http://members.aol.com/quinnp1/index.html). Peyton has a good background in martial arts and spent years as a bouncer, where he learned to handle the various threat levels we've discussed. (Call him for your drunk brother-in-law at the wedding.) He's also survived knife and other weapon attacks, including three armed robberies. Add that to the beauty of the Rocky Mountains, and you should have fun at the same time you're learning.

W. Hock Hochheim's Scientific Street Fighting Congress for Modern Tactical Hand, Stick, and Knife Combat/Chief Instructor: Hock Hochheim, P.O. Box 292373, Lewisville, TX 75029 (Web site: http://www.americanknifefighters.com). Hock's a retired "flatfoot" like me. He's been forced to put his learning to the test, and he's got the battle scars of 23 years on the street to prove it. The result is a great program. He also travels extensively giving seminars.

Warrior Arts Center/Chief Instructor: J. Bear Street, 3217 B Concordia Ave., Monroe, LA 71201. Bear is another old "martial arts bum" who has served his time in the traditional styles so you won't have to if you don't want to. He'll teach you no-nonsense, practical defense. (He's also a great tattoo artist if you're interested. Get away from *me* with that needle, Bear!)

Worden's Combative Arts: Natural Spirit International/Chief Instructor: Kelly Worden, P.O. Box 64069, Tacoma, WA 98464. Kelly is another old 30-plus year martial arts war horse who earned the right to be called master in several traditional arts, took that training, then turned it into a practical system for today's streets called Connecting the Systems. Sponsor of the annual Natural Spirit Water and Steel training retreat on Raft Island, Washington.

If you are forced to start from scratch to find good training, visit a variety of programs and observe classes carefully before enrolling. Beware of long-term contracts; anything up to six months or so is reasonable, but I'd stay away from longer commitments—you may well find yourself a victim of a "snow job" and wish to look elsewhere. Ask the chief instructor direct questions about self-defense, and find out if modern weapons are part of the curriculum. Above all, avoid American instructors who speak broken English, leaving out articles of speech like *a* and *the*. (They won't say, "This is a good school," like most people born in this country would. It'll be, "This is good school," spoken with a phony Japanese accent.) They also divide their living rooms into little cubicles with *shoji* screens, make you bow and take your shoes off when you enter their house, and if they invite you over for dinner you'll have to kneel on the floor and eat sushi with chopsticks. I call these guys Ki Zombies—they've totally entered their dream worlds and think they were samurai warriors and *kamikaze* pilots in earlier incarnations.

Now, sure as I live and breath, about a week after this book comes out someone I haven't talked to for awhile, didn't know was still teaching, or otherwise overlooked when preparing this list is going to give me an irritated call. So I'll just slap my forehead and apologize in advance. As I said, there are more good teachers out there than those I've listed. Seek, with wisdom, and ye shall find what you're looking for.

Not any profane man, not any sensual, not any liar, not any slave can teach, but only he can give who has.

—R.W. Emerson
Address to the Divinity College
Cambridge, MA, July 15, 1838

Conclusion

Beyond Technique

Put it before them briefly so they will read it, clearly so they will appreciate it, picturesquely so they will remember it and, above all, accurately so they will be guided by its light.
—Joseph Pulitzer

Thanks, Joe. I've tried to follow your advice in writing *Real World Self-Defense*, because it really does bother me that evil-but-stronger people sometimes hurt good-but-weaker people. In many ways, I guess, I'm still that schoolboy on the playground who always felt it was his responsibility to step in when some bully was picking on a weaker kid. About the only real change is that I've learned that I can't be on every "playground" everywhere, all the time, for all people.

In any book, there are things the writer wants, and even feels he needs, to bring out but which never really seem to find their way into the "flow" of the manuscript. Self-defense—particularly the emotional and psychological aspects—is just too multifaceted to cover in any book, or any number of books. It's a lot like the legendary Greek hydra who, when one of his heads was cut off, immediately grew seven new ones: each mental aspect of the warrior mind-set that is conquered opens new doors to new questions that must be contemplated and resolved. And each question is a little different for each individual. So the subject goes beyond that of which the printed, or even the spoken, word is capable. For that reason, every man and woman must deal with these questions individually and internally. And each must recognize it as an ongoing process that has no end.

Successfully defending yourself is the result of about 99 percent psychological and emotional preparation and 1 percent training. Unfortunately, most people, even dedicated students of the martial arts, take the opposite approach by spending the vast majority of their time trying to master complex and impractical techniques or in a futile quest for perfect form. If they think about the warrior mind-set at all, they assume it will develop on its own as a result of their physical training. That's not going to happen. Students must develop it on their own.

I hope you have found my personal view of self-defense both helpful and entertaining, and I hope that it can add to your body of knowledge on the subject. I have tried to write this book for two audiences. The first consists of those who have already developed the correct mind-set—be they martial artists, police officers, military personnel, or merely civilians who, like Margaret in our opening chapter, have faced the reality of a violent society and chosen to be survivors rather than victims.

To you warriors, I would encourage continued study, both mental and physical, and advocate that you explore new disciplines, philosophies, and ideas rather than stick defiantly to one teacher, school of thought, or style of fighting. If you have not already done so, sooner or later you will realize that while martial arts are not religion, they share many aspects with it. You might be a Baptist, Catholic, Methodist, or Presbyterian, but unless you follow every infinitesimal tenet of that theology, you actually have your own personal denomination within your heart. Your beliefs are just a little different from those of every other member of your faith. So it goes with fighting styles; no two people punch or kick exactly alike. Practice karate, aikido, or arnis. Box, wrestle, or study savate. Or train at one of the modern combat schools if you like. You will still develop your own personal method of self-defense upon which you must rely. Your biggest enemy is ignoring this fact and trying to become a carbon copy of your instructor or some other fighter you respect. It can't be done, and it is destructive to attempt.

The second group for whom this book is written comprises those who recognize a need to defend themselves in today's society but have not yet learned how, mentally or physically. I hope to inspire you to pursue a successful course of study in both areas. There is an old joke that asks, "What is the definition of a conservative?" The answer is, "A liberal who got mugged last night." There is actually much truth for us here, as most people do not recognize a need for defensive competence until they, or someone close to them, have suffered the consequences of not possessing such skills. You can save yourself a lot of grief if you acknowledge this necessity ahead of time. To paraphrase an old cliché, "Close the barn door before the cow is gone."

The Chinese call it yin and yang; to the Japanese it's en-yo. It's a concept that is not unique to the Orient, however. It's also found in the Viking rune Dagaz, and many other Western warrior cultures. It's male/female, day/night, up/down, right/left, and life and death. Many of us in modern society perceive this concept as "opposites." We should really view it more as *balance*. You can call it anything you like, or nothing at all, but one of its precepts is that there are times when you should be polite and passive and other times when you must be aggressive—aggressive to the point of ruthlessness if that's what the situation calls for.

This has not been an easy book for me to write. When writing any instructional book, the author always wonders how he might have misstated himself, or how he might be misinterpreted. That's not so bad if you're instructing people in how to buy a lawn mower, or telling them which plastic trash bags are best, or advising men not to wear white shoes after Labor Day. When teaching people to defend themselves, however, you constantly live under the pressure that your mistake could cost someone his or her life.

But there's another reason this book has been a tough one. Between the inception of *Real World Self-Defense* and the completion of the final draft, I have lost the three men who taught me the most about self-defense, the warrior mind-set, and life in general.

During the outlining phase of this book, my undercover training officer, Sid Cookerly, suffered a fatal heart attack. Sid taught me far more than just how to be an effective undercover police officer—he taught me how to stay alive while working around some of society's most dangerous excuses for human beings. From Sid I learned the casual glance, the angry frown, the icy stare; body language that very subtly conveyed the message, "I will kill anyone stupid enough to mess with me." Such techniques may very well have saved my life without my ever knowing it.

Sid also taught me advanced shooting techniques, and we spent long hours discussing knife, stick, and unarmed combat, and the resolution it takes to bridge the abyss between theory and reality. It was a vital period in the development of my own warrior mind-set.

Then things got worse. One of the greatest honors I've ever had was when Col. Rex Applegate agreed to write one of the two Forewords I originally planned for *Real World Self-Defense*. I have already mentioned and quoted the Colonel numerous times in this text, but for anyone not familiar with him, he was, among many other things, considered the foremost authority on close-quarters combat. You may remember that I was first introduced to his name by my uncle who taught me to point shoot, and becoming close friends with the Colonel as an adult was one of the highlights of my life. If you're my age or older, think of what it would have been like to get phone calls every Friday afternoon from Roy Rogers. If you're younger, imagine Arnold Schwarzenegger inviting you to come spend a few days at his house. I never got over the awe of being friends with a man who had been one of my childhood heros.

At the age of 84, Colonel Applegate was still vital, alert, and active. But as I was completing the rough draft of this book and preparing to send him a copy, I received a phone call telling me he had been rushed to the hospital. The stroke he had suffered appeared to have been successfully treated, and I was lucky enough to speak with him one last time on the phone. But complications soon arose, and on August 14, 1998, the world lost a great warrior—and an even greater human being.

But the worst was yet to come.

I was in the process of putting the final touches on this book when my father died. He had been on kidney dialysis for more than six years, and I had watched the health of this man who had once played tackle for the Philadelphia Eagles steadily fail, until he lay in bed unable to move. But he fought his invisible assailants to the end, never losing his spirit, sense of humor, or the love he had for God, his family, and friends. It had been many years since I had come to terms with the fact that he and I were different and destined to follow very different paths in very different ways. Since that time, our relationship had deepened, and I had finally come to the point where when he said, "I'm proud of you," I could accept it as coming from his heart rather than just being a smokescreen for disappointment that I had not followed in his footsteps.

I am left now with the comforting knowledge that he has joined my mother, and many pleasant memories. Among those memories, forever frozen in my mind, will be the remembrance of my very first self-defense lesson when I was 4 years old. Dad came home from work one night with two brand new pairs of boxing gloves, and I will never forget the smile on his face when he'd tap me a little too hard; I'd shake it off and come back swinging. Many years later, Grandpa Leon would sit on the couch in my living room with that same smile while I gave my own 4-year-old son his first lesson with the same, now-well-worn, gloves.

It was if, somehow, the cycle had been completed.

Yin and yang. En-yo. Dagaz. Death is not the opposite of life; it is part of it. And it will come to us all someday. But it should come when God calls for it, not when some filthy street maggot decides your watch, ring, and money are more valuable than you are. The recent deaths of these three men—my father and two men who served as father figures—have pushed me on down the road of my own life, and further away from the fear of death. When it is time, it will come. But I will allow no one to steal it from me prematurely—at least not without one hell of a fight first.

Just as between daylight and night there is dusk, and in the same sense that some nights the moon is brighter and some days the clouds hide the sun, there are various shades of danger facing all of us as the

20th century closes and the 21st begins. My guess is that it's going to get worse before it gets better. Restrictive government, civil unrest, disease, terrorism, and natural disasters continue to increase. You can survive them, but it will take preparation—especially mental preparation in the form of developing the warrior mind-set. Whether you face a lone assailant or a society gone to shambles, you must have decided in advance that you will do whatever must be done, pleasant or not, without hesitation.

In the same sense that Joseph Pulitzer's words at the beginning of this final chapter were what I aspired for when I began *Real World Self-Defense*, it is my hope that the words of Samuel Johnson that end the book will fit my final product. Only you can be the judge of that, so again, one final time, in self-defense and every other aspect of life, think for yourself. Trust your instincts and intuitions, and once committed to a course of action, never deviate from that course. As the great Satchel Page said, "Don't look back. Something might be gaining on you."

I wish you well.

I knew very well what I was undertaking, and very well how to do it, and have done it very well.

—Samuel Johnson
Boswell's Life, 1779

Appendix

References and Resources

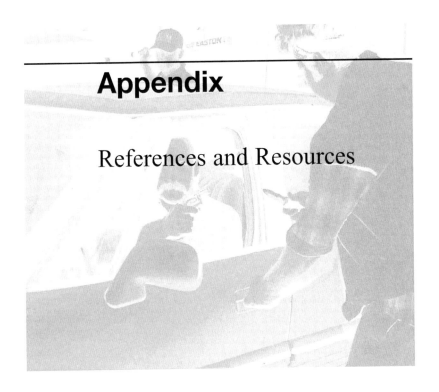

Following are some of the references and resources I've found to be helpful and enlightening. Again, the list is far from complete; it includes only the products or companies with which I am personally acquainted. However, I strongly suggest obtaining a copy of the Paladin Press catalog (or visit the Web site at www.paladin-press.com), since Paladin is the best source for this type of material.

REFERENCE BOOKS

Combat Use of the Double-Edged Fighting Knife, Col. Rex Applegate, Paladin Press, Boulder, CO.

Bullseyes Don't Shoot Back, Col. Rex Applegate and Michael Janich, Paladin Press, Boulder, CO.

Fast and Fancy Revolver Shooting, Ed McGivern, New Win Publishing, Inc., Clinton, NJ.

Guns, Bullets, and Gunfights, Jim Cirillo, Paladin Press, Boulder, CO.

Get Tough, Capt. W.E. Fairbairn, Paladin Press, Boulder, CO.

Handgun Stopping Power and *Street Stoppers*, Evan P. Marshall and Edwin J. Sanow, Paladin Press, Boulder, CO.

Kill or Get Killed, Col. Rex Applegate, Paladin Press, Boulder, CO.

Knife Fighting: A Practical Course, Michael Janich, Paladin Press, Boulder, CO.

Knife Fighting Encyclopedia, Hock Hochheim, Lauric Press, Lewisville, TX.

The Martial Artist's Book of Five Rings, Miyamoto Musashi, translated by Steve Kaufman, Charles E. Tuttle Company, Inc., Boston, MA.

No Second Place Winner, Bill Jordan, Police Bookshelf, Concord, NH.

Sharpening the Warrior's Edge, Bruce Siddle, PPCT Research Publications, Millstadt, IL.

Quick or Dead, William L. Cassidy, Paladin Press, Boulder, CO.

Shooting To Live, W.E. Fairbairn and E.A. Sykes, Paladin Press, Boulder, CO.

Street Steel: Choosing and Carrying Self-Defense Knives, Michael Janich, Paladin Press, Boulder, CO.

The Working Folding Knife, Dick, Stoeger Publishing Co., Wayne, NJ.

TRAINING VIDEOTAPE SOURCES

Combat Technologies (COMTECH), Milton-Freewater, OR. Anything you get from these folks will be as good as it comes. Keating and his instructors have "been there, done that" on the street as well as in the training hall. Check out the Web site (www.combattech.com) for a complete list of both general and highly specialized weapon and unarmed combat videos.

Worden's Combative Arts, Natural Spirit International, Tacoma, WA. (Web site: http://home.earthlink.net/~wordenk/.) Kelly Worden grew up in a "tough neighborhood," to put it mildly. He's my age and still alive, and that should speak for itself. Natural Spirit has its own videos, which cut through the "bovine excrement" and get right to the point.

W. Hock Hochheim's Scientific Street Fighting Congress for Modern Tactical Hand, Stick, and Knife Combat, Lewisville, TX. (Web site: www.americanknifefighters.com.) Hock has an extensive line of practical videos that come as a result of years of martial arts training combined with hundreds, if not thousands, of actual street encounters during his 23 years as a cop.

International Combat Hapkido Federation, Plantation, FL. This is your source for John Pelligrini's cane defense tape, mentioned earlier in the text.

CUSTOM KNIFE MAKERS AND/OR DESIGNERS

Bill Bagwell, P.O. Box 315, Crowville, LA 71230.

Black Cloud Knives, 5900 West Venus Way, Chandler, AZ 85226.

Frank Centofante, P.O. Box 928, Madisonville, TN 37354.

Pat Crawford, 205 N. Center Drive, West Memphis, AR 72301.

Bob Dozier, P.O. Box 1941, Springdale, AR 72765.

Ernest Emerson, 4142 W. 173rd Street, Torrence, CA 90504.

Bram Frank (Diverse Marketing), 4430 Old Colony Road, Mulberry, FL 33860.

William W. Harsey, 82710 N. Howe Lane, Creswell, OR 97426.

Newt Livesay (Wicked Knife Co.), 202 Rains Road, Siloam Springs, AR 72761.

Bob Lum, 901 Travis Ave., Eugene, OR 97404.

Ken Onion, 91-990 Oaniani Street, Capolei, HI 96707.

Randall Made Knives, P.O. Box 1988, Orlando, FL 32802.

Chris Reeves, 11624 W. President Drive, Apt. B, Boise, ID 83713.

Round Eye Knife & Tool, P.O. Box 818, Sagle, ID 83860.

Ruby Mountain Knife Works, P.O. Box 534, Twin Bridges, MT 59754.

Tony Stephens, 3632 Equestrian Court, Edmond, OK 73034.

Szabo, Inc., 13283 SW 124th Steet, Miami, FL, 33186.

Bob Terzuola, Rt. 6, Box 83-A, Santa Fe, NM 87501.

PRODUCTION KNIFE COMPANIES

Al Mar Knives, 5755 SW Jean Road, Suite 101, Lake Oswego, OR 97035.

Benchmade Knife Co., Inc., 300 Beaver Creek Road, Oregon City, OR 97045.

Boker USA, Inc., 1550 Balsam Street, Lakewood, CO 80215.

Cold Steel, Inc., 2128-D Knoll Drive, Ventura, CA 93003.

Columbia River Knife & Tool, 9720 SW Hillman Court, Suite 805, Wilsonville, OR 97070.

Gerber Legendary Blades, P.O. Box 23088, 14200 SW 72nd Ave., Portland, OR 97281.

Ontario Knife Co., P.O. Box 145, Franklinville, NY 14737.

SOG Specialty Knives, P.O. Box 1024, Edmonds, WA 98020.

Spyderco, Inc., P.O. Box 800, Golden, CO 80402.

OTHER PRODUCTS

ASP (collapsible batons, pepper sprays, and other defense items), 2511 E. Capital Dr., Appleton, WI 54911.

The Barami Corporation (Hip-Grip Pistol Handle Holder), 6689 Orchard Lake Road #148, West Bloomfield, MI 48322.

Crossman Corporation (pellet revolvers and semiautos), Routes 5 & 20, East Bloomfield, NY 14443.

Gamo (pellet revolvers and semiautos), 6821 SW Archer Road, Gainsville, FL 32608.

Handgun Concealment/Jagwear Concealment Systems (quality briefcases, camera bags, etc.), 40 Kitty Hawk East, Richmond, TX 77469.

About the Author

Over the past 30 years, Jerry VanCook has trained thousands of police officers, military personnel, and civilians in both armed and unarmed defense. An instructor in Okinawan karate, he has studied aikido, Thai boxing, kung fu, and kali, and he recently received his Rokudan (6th-degree Black Belt) ranking in Bei-Koku Aibujutsu. In 1998 he was inducted into the World Head of Family Sokeship International Martial Arts Hall of Fame and received the "Writer of the Year" award. He is also a certified National Rifle Association firearms and personal protection instructor.

Fourteen years in law enforcement with the Garfield County, Oklahoma, Sheriff's Department, a federally funded undercover task force, and the Oklahoma State Bureau of Investigation, as well as what he sometimes refers to as a "misspent youth," taught VanCook the difference between practical self-defense and the sport and art aspects of dojo training.

VanCook is the author of *Going Undercover: Secrets and Sound Advice for the Undercover Officer* (Paladin Press) and more than 30 novels in the *Executioner*, *Stony Man Farm*, and *Super Bolan* series featuring Mack Bolan (Gold Eagle Books). He is a contributing editor to *Tactical Knives*, has written for *Filipino Martial Arts* and *Combat Knives*, and writes the "Trail's Edge" column (edged weaponry of the Old West) for *Trail's End* magazine.

He is shown here with two of his favorite personal defense weapons, the Taurus Model 608 and the Applegate-Fairbairn Smatchet.